Math in Focus®

Singapore Math®
by Marshall Cavendish

Student Edition

Program Consultant and Author
Dr. Fong Ho Kheong

Authors
Gan Kee Soon
Chelvi Ramakrishnan

 **Marshall Cavendish** Education

U.S. Distributor

Houghton Mifflin Harcourt.
The Learning Company™

Grade **4B**

Contents

Area and Perimeter

Chapter Opener

How do you find the perimeter and area of a rectangle or square using a formula?
How do you find an unknown side of a rectangle or square given its area or perimeter?

RECALL PRIOR KNOWLEDGE

Understanding and finding the perimeter of a figure • Finding an unknown side given the perimeter • Understanding and finding area of a figure

• Finding the area of a square or rectangle by multiplying its side lengths

• Finding area of a figure by separating it into rectangles

▶ Hands-on Activity

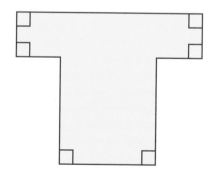

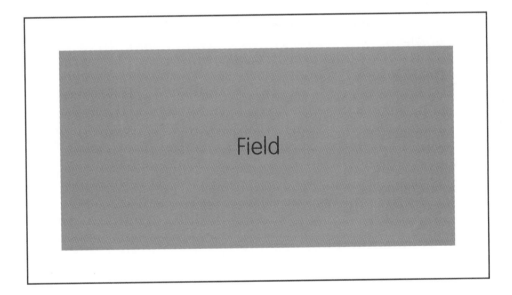

7 Angles and Line Segments

Chapter Opener

How can you measure and draw angles?
How can you draw perpendicular and parallel line segments?

RECALL PRIOR KNOWLEDGE

Defining a point, a line, and a line segment • Defining angles • Comparing angles with a right angle • Checking perpendicular lines • Checking parallel lines • Finding perpendicular and/or parallel lines

 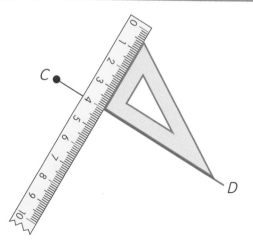
Hands-on Activity

Polygons and Symmetry

Chapter Opener 255

How do you sort and classify polygons?
How can you identify symmetric shapes and patterns?

RECALL PRIOR KNOWLEDGE 256

Identifying polygons • Identifying quadrilaterals • Combining plane shapes
to form other plane shapes

▶ Hands-on Activity

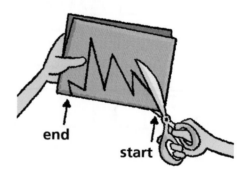

end

start

Tables and Line Graphs

Chapter Opener

How can you use a table or a line graph to represent, organize, and interpret information?
How do you choose an appropriate graph to show information?

RECALL PRIOR KNOWLEDGE

Reading numbers from a number line • Finding parts of a whole •
Interpreting data in a picture graph • Interpreting data in a bar graph

▶ Hands-on Activity

© 2020 Marshall Cavendish Education Pte Ltd

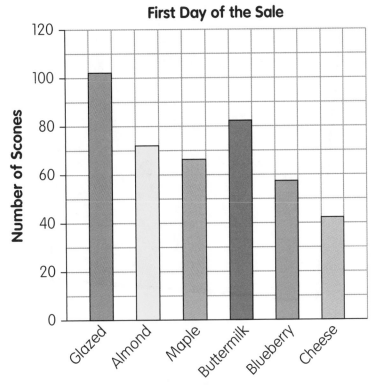

Manipulative List

Protractors

Preface

Welcome!

Math in Focus® is a program that puts **you** at the center of an exciting learning experience! This experience is all about helping you to build skills and math ideas that make sense, sharing your thinking to deepen your understanding, and learning to become a strong and confident problem solver!

What's in your book?

Each chapter in this book begins with a real-world example of the math topic you are about to learn.

In each chapter, you will see the following features:

THINK introduces a problem for the whole section, to get you thinking creatively and critically. You may not be able to answer the problem right away but you can come back to it a few times as you work through the section.

ENGAGE introduces tasks that link what you already know with what you will be learning next. The tasks will have you exploring and discussing math concepts with your classmates.

LEARN introduces you to new math concepts through a Concrete-Pictorial-Abstract (C-P-A) approach, using examples and activities.

Hands-on Activity provides you with the experience of working very closely with your classmates. These Hands-On Activities allow you to become more confident in what you have learned and help you to uncover new concepts.

TRY provides you with the opportunity to practice what you are learning, with support and guidance.

INDEPENDENT PRACTICE allows you to work on different kinds of problems and apply the concepts and skills you have learned to solve these problems on your own.

Additional features include:

RECALL PRIOR KNOWLEDGE	Math Talk	MATH SHARING	GAME
Helps you recall related concepts you learned before, accompanied by practice questions	Invites you to explain your reasoning and communicate your ideas to your classmates and teachers	Encourages you to create strategies, discover methods, and share them with your classmates and teachers using mathematical language	Helps you to really master the concepts you learned, through fun partner games
LET'S EXPLORE	**MATH JOURNAL**	**PUT ON YOUR THINKING CAP!**	**CHAPTER WRAP-UP**
Extends your learning through investigation	Allows you to reflect on your learning when you write down your thoughts about the concepts learned	Challenges you to apply the concepts to solve problems in different ways	Summarizes your learning in a flow chart and helps you to make connections within the chapter
CHAPTER REVIEW	**Assessment Prep**	**PERFORMANCE TASK**	**STEAM**
Provides you with a lot of practice in the concepts learned	Prepares you for state tests with assessment-type problems	Assesses your learning through problems that allow you to demonstrate your understanding and knowledge	Promotes collaboration with your classmates through interesting projects that allow you to use math in creative ways

Let's begin your exciting learning journey with us! Are you ready?

Chapter 5

Conversion of Measurements

How can you measure length, mass, weight, volume, and time in different units?

Name: _____ Date: _____

Measuring and comparing length in meters and centimeters

The meter is a unit of length. It is used to measure longer lengths and heights.

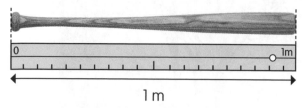

1 m

The baseball bat is 1 meter long.

The cupboard is 2 meters tall.

The centimeter is also a unit of length.
It is used to measure shorter lengths.

The pencil is 15 centimeters long.

▶ **Quick Check**

Find the length of each object.

1 The garbage can is _____ meter tall.

2 The ribbon is _____ centimeters long.

Find the difference between the lengths of the crayon and the eraser.

3

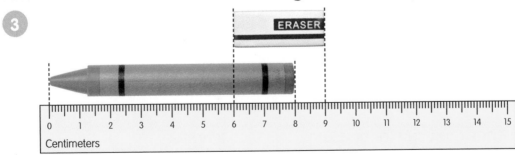

The difference between the lengths is _____ centimeters.

Measuring and estimating lengths in feet and inches

Both feet (ft) and inches (in.) are customary units of length.

1 foot (ft) = 12 inches (in.)

Feet are used to measure longer lengths.
Inches are used to measure shorter lengths.
Inch-rulers are used for measuring customary lengths.

The paper clip is an inch long.

The math book is less than
10 inches long.

The height of the chair is
more than 3 feet.

▶ Quick Check

Fill in each blank with shorter **or** longer.

4 Feet are used to measure _____ lengths.

5 Inches are used to measure _____ lengths.

Name two objects for each measure.

6 About 1 inch long _____

7 More than 1 foot long _____

8 Less than one foot long _____

Choose the correct unit of measure for each object.
Fill in each blank with inches or feet.

9

10

_____   _____

Measuring mass in kilograms and grams

The watermelon has a mass of 2 kilograms 300 grams. What is the mass of the watermelon in grams?

$$2 \text{ kg } 300 \text{ g} < \begin{array}{l} 2 \text{ kg} = 2{,}000 \text{ g} \\ 300 \text{ g} \end{array}$$

$$2 \text{ kg } 300 \text{ g} = 2{,}000 \text{ g} + 300 \text{ g}$$
$$= 2{,}300 \text{ g}$$

The mass of the watermelon is 2,300 grams.

▶ Quick Check

Read each scale to find the mass. Then, write each mass in grams.

⑪

⑫

_____ kg _____ g

= _____ g + _____ g

= _____ g

_____ kg _____ g

= _____ g + _____ g

= _____ g

Measuring volume in liters and milliliters

A carton of juice is completely filled with orange juice.
The orange juice is emptied into measuring cups.
Find the capacity of the carton in milliliters.

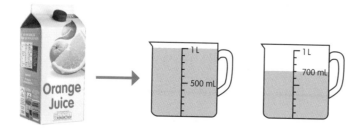

1 L 700 mL $\left\{\begin{array}{l} 1\ L = 1{,}000\ mL \\ 700\ mL \end{array}\right.$

1 L 700 mL = 1,000 mL + 700 mL
        = 1,700 mL

The capacity of the carton of 1,700 milliliters.

▶ **Quick Check**

Write the capacity in milliliters.

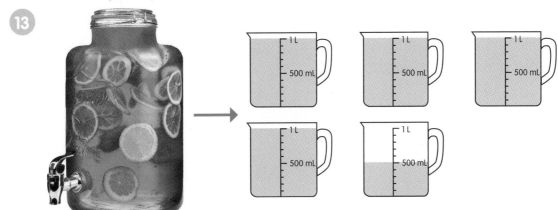

The capacity of the water dispenser is _____ litres _____ milliliters.

_____ L _____ mL = _____ mL + _____ mL

= _____ mL

Converting hours to minutes

Robert painted a picture for 1 hour 24 minutes. How many minutes did he paint?

1 h 24 min = 60 min + 24 min
       = 84 min

1 h 24 min $\Big<$ 1 h = 60 min
                24 min

Robert painted for 84 minutes.

▶ **Quick Check**

Write each time in minutes.

14 1 h 52 min = _____ min + _____ min

= _____ min

15 6 h 36 min = _____ min + _____ min

= _____ min

Solve one-step real-world problems involving measurement

Simone made 6 liters 860 milliliters of juice for a party. There were 940 milliliters of juice leftover. How much juice was drunk at the party? Give your answer in milliliters.

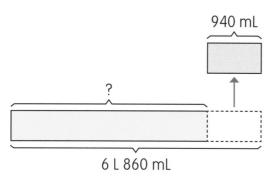

6 L 860 mL = 6,000 mL + 860 mL
                = 6,860 mL

6,860 − 940 = 5,920

5,920 milliliters of juice were drunk at the party.

▶ Quick Check

Solve.

16 The mass of a bag of flour is 3 kilograms 26 grams. The mass of a pineapple is 986 grams. What is the total mass of the bag of flour and pineapple in grams?

Length in Customary Units

Learning Objectives:
- Measure and estimate length in customary units.
- Convert between different units of measurement of length.

New Vocabulary
yard (yd)
distance
mile (mi)

THINK

Axel says 1 yard is 3 feet. Zara says 1 yard is 36 inches. Who is correct? Why?

ENGAGE

a Study a ruler that measures in inches. How many inches are there on the ruler?
b Now, draw a line that is shorter than the length of the ruler. How many inches long is the line that you drew? How many centimeters long is that? How do you know? Explain your thinking.

LEARN Measure length in feet and inches

1 The picture frame is 1 foot long. It is 12 inches long.

2 Mr. Williams is 6 feet tall. What is his height in inches?
You can use a table to relate feet and inches.

Foot (ft)	Inch (in.)
1	12
2	24
3	36
4	48
5	60
6	72

1 ft = 12 in.

2 ft = 2 × 12 = 24 in.

3 ft = 3 × 12 = 36 in.

4 ft = 4 × 12 = 48 in.

5 ft = 5 × 12 = 60 in.

6 ft = 6 × 12 = 72 in.

Mr. Williams' height is 72 inches.

TRY Practice measuring length in feet and inches

Write each length in inches. You can use a table to help.

1 3 ft = _____ ◯ _____

= _____ in.

2 7 ft = _____ ◯ _____

= _____ in.

Compare each pair of lengths. Write >, <, or =.

3 6 ft ◯ 70 in.

4 48 in. ◯ 4 ft

TRY Practice measuring length in yards

Estimate the height of the cupboard to the nearest yard.

1

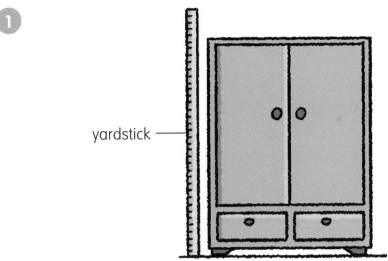

yardstick

The height of the cupboard is about _____ yard(s).

Estimate the length of each object to the nearest yard.

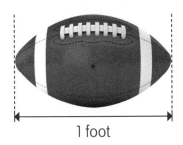

1 foot

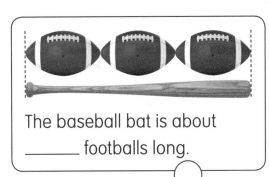

The baseball bat is about _____ footballs long.

2 The length of the baseball bat is about _____ yard.

3 The length of a car is about _____ yards.

Fill in each blank with taller or shorter.

4 A chair is _____ than 3 yards.

5 A house is _____ than 2 yards.

Write each length in feet or inches.

6 2 yd = _____ ft

7 3 yd = _____ in.

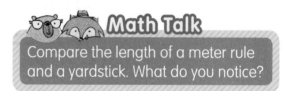

Yard (yd)	Feet (ft)
1	3
2	
3	

Compare each pair of lengths. Write >, <, or =.

8 9 ft ◯ 3 yd

9 5 yd ◯ 150 in.

Math Talk

Compare the length of a meter rule and a yardstick. What do you notice?

ENGAGE

Measure the length of your stride in feet. Walk along the length of your classroom. Estimate the length of the classroom in feet.
How can you write its length in another way? Share your ideas with your partner.

LEARN Measure length in miles

1 The standard customary unit for measuring distance is the mile.
mi stands for mile.

The distance you can briskly walk in 20 minutes is about 1 mile.

1 mile (mi) = 1,760 yards (yd)
1 mile (mi) = 5,280 feet (ft)

1 yd = 3 ft

2

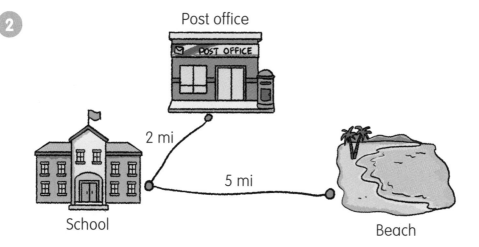

Post office

School

Beach

2 mi

5 mi

The distance between the school and the post office is 2 miles.
Is the school about 3,500 yards from the post office?

Yes. The post office is also about 10,000 feet away from the school.

The distance between the school and the beach is 5 miles.
Is the school about 5,000 yards from the beach?

No. It is farther than 5,000 yards away. It is 5 miles. So, it is 8,800 yards from the beach.

TRY Practice measuring length in miles

Fill in each blank.

1. A helicopter is flying at a height of 5,257 feet.

   It is about _____ mile high.

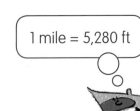

1 mile = 5,280 ft

2. Rebeca estimated the distance between her home and the school to be about 1 mile.

Rebeca's house   School

Give two possible distances in feet that are about 1 mile.

They are _____ and _____.

3. A 3-mile brisk walk will usually take about _____ minutes.

Write each length in yards or feet.

4. 2 mi = _____ × _____

   = _____ yd

5. 3 mi = _____ × _____

   = _____ ft

Fill in the blank with greater than or less than.

6. A bus traveled 9 miles from Town A to Town B. It then traveled 15,000 yards from Town B to Town C.

   The distance between Town A and Town B is _____ the distance between Town B and Town C.

INDEPENDENT PRACTICE

Choose the unit you would use to measure each object.
Use inch, foot, yard, or mile.

1 the length of a pair of glasses _____

2 the length of a football field _____

Underline the best estimate of each object.

3 The length of two footballs is about 2 (inches / feet / yards / miles).

4 The distance a person might travel to school is about
2 (inches / feet / yards / miles).

Circle the object that is about 1 yard long.

5

Bottle

Belt

House

Fill in each blank.

6 A wooden board is 4 feet long. Express the length in inches.

The length of the wooden board is _____ inches.

7 A plant grew 1 yard in a year. How many inches did the plant grow
that year?

The plant grew _____ inches that year.

Solve.

8 Mateo cycled 3 miles one morning. Tiana cycled 5,000 yards that same morning. Who cycled a shorter distance?

9 Aubrey has some fabric that is 12 feet long. She needs 5 yards of fabric to make curtains. Does she have enough fabric?

2 Weight and Volume in Customary Units

Learning Objectives:
- Estimate and measure weight and volume in customary units
- Read scales in customary units
- Convert between different units of measurement of weight and volume

New Vocabulary

ounce (oz)	pound (lb)
ton (T)	cup (c)
pint (pt)	fluid ounce (fl oz)
quart (qt)	gallon (gal)

THINK

a Estimate the weight of your school bag. What are the different units you can use? How are the units related?

b Estimate the amount of water you drink in a day. What are the different units you can use? How are the units related?

ENGAGE

Take some weights.

a Use a balance to find how many of these weights can balance a pencil.

b Without measuring, estimate the weight of an inch ruler using the weights.

LEARN Estimate and measure weight in ounces

1. The **ounce** is a customary unit of weight.
It is used for measuring light objects.
oz stands for ounce.

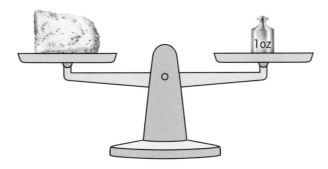

The balance shows the weight of 1 slice of bread.
The weight of the slice of bread is about 1 ounce.

2 A slice of bread weighs about 1 ounce.
You can use the slice of bread to estimate
the weights of other light objects.

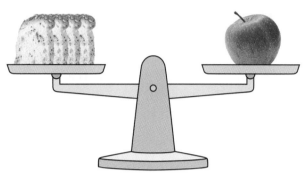

1 slice of bread weighs
about 1 ounce. 4 slices
of bread weigh about
4 ounces.

The weight of the apple is about 4 ounces.

3 The balance shows the weight of some carrots.

The weight of the carrots is 8 ounces.

4

The pointer on the
scale is nearer to
the 3-ounce mark.

The orange weighs more than 3 ounces but
less than 4 ounces.

The orange weighs about 3 ounces.

5 The apples weigh more than 9 ounces but less than 10 ounces.

The pointer on the scale is nearer to the 10-ounce mark.

The apples weigh about 10 ounces.

Hands-on Activity Estimating and measuring weight in ounces

Work in pairs.

① Guess the weight of each object in ounces. Fill in the column "Estimate" in the table.

Object	Estimate	Actual Weight (oz)
MATH Your math book		
A marker pen		
A whiteboard eraser		
Two file folders		

② Measure each object with a scale in ounces. Record your answers in the table in ①.

TRY Practice estimating and measuring weight in ounces

Fill in each blank.

1 A slice of cheese weighs about 1 ounce.

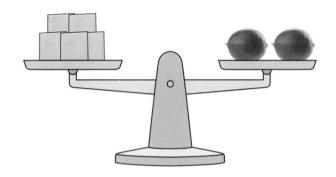

The weight of 2 limes is about _____ ounces.

2 The weight of 3 apples is _____ ounces.

3 The weight of the tube of toothpaste is about _____ ounces.

4 The weight of two tennis balls is about _____ ounces.

ENGAGE

Take some weights.
a Use a balance to find how many of these weights can balance 2 math books.
b Without measuring, can you tell how many of these weights can balance the weight of a watermelon?

LEARN Estimate and measure weight in pounds

1 The pound is another customary unit of weight.
It is used for measuring heavy objects.
lb stands for pound.

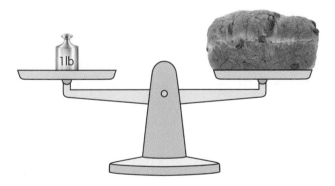

The scale shows the weight of 1 loaf of bread.
The weight of a loaf of bread is about 1 pound.

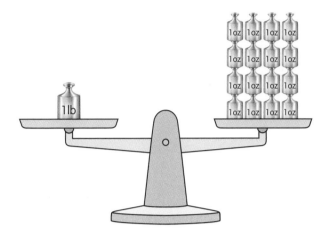

1 pound (lb) = 16 ounces (oz)

2

The pointer on the scale is closer to the 2-pound mark.

The bananas weigh more than 2 pounds but less than 3 pounds.

The bananas weigh about 2 pounds.

3

The fish and shrimp weigh more than 13 pounds and less than 14 pounds.

The fish and shrimp weigh about 14 pounds.

> The pointer is at the mark halfway between 13 pounds and 14 pounds.

4 The weight of some lemons is 2 pounds.
What is the weight of the lemons in ounces?

2 lb = 2 × 16
    = 32 oz

The weight of the lemons is 32 ounces.

Work in pairs.

Activity 1 Estimating and measuring weight in pounds

① Guess the weight of each object in pounds. Fill in the column "Estimate" in the table.

Object	Estimate	Actual Weight (lb)
Your school bag		
A stack of 2 books		
4 bottles of water		

② Measure each object with a scale in pounds. Record the answers in the table in ①.

Activity 2 Naming objects measured in ounces and pounds

① Think of the different things you see in a supermarket.
Name three objects each that are measured in
a ounces.
b pounds.

TRY Practice estimating and measuring weight in pounds

Fill in each blank.

1

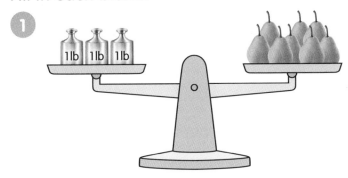

The pears weigh about _____ pounds.

2

The sack of potatoes

weighs _____ pounds.

3

The watermelon weighs

about _____ pounds.

4

The basket of tomatoes weighs about _____ pounds.

Write each weight in ounces.

5 8 lb = _____ × _____

= _____ oz

6 13 lb = _____ × _____

= _____ oz

Compare each pair of weights. Write >, <, or =.

7 2 lb ◯ 2 oz

8 18 oz ◯ 12 lb

9 4 lb ◯ 40 oz

10 128 oz ◯ 8 lb

Solve.

11 The weight of some chocolate bars is 4 pounds.
What is the weight of the chocolate bars in ounces?

© 2020 Marshall Cavendish Education Pte Ltd

ENGAGE

How many pounds do you think an African elephant weighs? How can you measure the weights of large things like elephants? Share your ideas with your partner.

LEARN Estimate and measure weight in tons

1 The ton is another customary unit of weight.
It is used for measuring very heavy objects.
T stands for ton.

1 ton = 2,000 lb

A car

A car weighs about 1 ton (T).

Which objects can be measured in tons?

An elephant, a whale, a helicopter, a polar bear …

A handful of mushrooms weighs about 8 ounces.
A bunch of grapes and a pineapple weigh about 4 pounds.
A large tractor weighs about 2 tons.

Customary Units of Weight

1 pound (lb) = 16 ounces (oz)
1 ton (T) = 2,000 pounds (lb)

2 A light aircraft weighs 6 tons. What is its weight in pounds?

$6 \text{ T} = 6 \times 2{,}000$

$= 12{,}000 \text{ lb}$

The weight of the light aircraft is 12,000 pounds.

TRY Practice estimating and measuring weight in tons

Choose the best unit to measure the weight of each object.
Use ounce, pound, or ton.

1 a bunch of bananas _____

2 a slice of cheese _____

3 a helicopter _____

4 a whale _____

Write each weight in pounds.

5 3 T = _____ × _____

= _____ lb

6 5 T = _____ × _____

= _____ lb

Compare each pair of weights. Write >, <, or =.

7 2,500 lb ◯ 1 T

8 3 T ◯ 7,900 lb

Solve.

9 A bus weighs 16 tons. What is its weight in pounds?

ENGAGE

A carton of orange juice contains 6 cups of juice. Wyatt pours the juice to fill 4 glasses completely. What is the capacity of each glass?

LEARN Estimate and measure volume in fluid ounces, cups, and pints

 The fluid ounce and cup are customary units for measuring volume.
fl oz stands for fluid ounce.
c stands for cup.

The capacity of the can is 16 fluid ounces.

The drink is completely poured into 2 cups.

2 cups (c) = 16 fluid ounces (fl oz)

1 cup (c) = 8 fluid ounces (fl oz)

② The pint is a customary unit for measuring volume. pt stands for pint.

The 2 cups are completely filled with water.
The 2 cups of water completely fill the pint carton.

1 pint (pt) = 2 cups (c)

The capacity of the carton is 1 pint.

1 pint of water is the same as 2 cups of water.

TRY Practice estimating and measuring volume in fluid ounces, cups, and pints

Fill in each blank.

1 The pitcher is completely filled with water.
The water is emptied into cups.

What is the capacity of the pitcher? _____ cups

2 Each carton contains 1 pint of milk.

The total amount of milk in the five cartons is _____ cups.

3 7 c = _____ × _____

= _____ fl oz

4 16 pt = _____ × _____

= _____ c

5 12 pt = _____ × _____

= _____ c

= _____ × _____

= _____ fl oz

Compare each pair of volumes. Write >, <, or =.

6 2 c ◯ 2 pt

7 1 pt ◯ 3 c

8 8 pt ◯ 128 fl oz

9 430 fl oz ◯ 19 pt

ENGAGE

3 pints of water can fill half of a pail. How many pints of water can fill 3 pails completely?

LEARN Estimate and measure volume in pints and quarts

1 The quart is a customary unit for measuring volume. qt stands for quart.

2 pints of milk can completely fill a bigger carton.

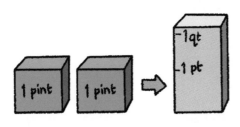

┌────────────────────────────────┐
│ 1 quart (qt) = 2 pints (pt)   │
└────────────────────────────────┘

The capacity of the bigger carton is 1 quart.

2 A container has 8 quarts of juice.
How many pints are there in 8 quarts?

8 qt = 8 × 2
     = 16 pt

There are 16 pints in 8 quarts.

3 A container is completely filled with 13 quarts of water. What is its capacity in cups?

13 qt = 13 × 2
    = 26 pt
    = 26 × 2
    = 52 c

1 qt = 2 pt
1 pt = 2 c
13 qt = ? c

The capacity of the container is 52 cups.

Hands-on Activity

Work in groups.

Activity 1 Estimating and measuring volume in pints and quarts

(1) This carton has a capacity of 1 pint. 1 pint

(2) Estimate the capacity of the pitcher given by your teacher.

Pitcher

(3) Fill up small cartons with water from the pitcher until the pitcher is empty.

(4) What is the capacity of the pitcher in pints? _____

What is the capacity of the pitcher in quarts? _____

Activity 2 Measuring capacity in cups and pints

(1) Bring some empty containers from your home.

(2) Find the capacity of each container with some cups or 1-pint cartons.

TRY Practice estimating and measuring volume in pints and quarts

Fill in each blank.

1 10 qt = _____ × _____

   = _____ pt

2 21 qt = _____ × _____

   = _____ c

3 32 qt = _____ × _____

   = _____ pt

   = _____ × _____

   = _____ c

Compare each pair of volumes. Write >, <, or =.

4 4 qt ◯ 2 pt

5 8 c ◯ 2 qt

Solve.

6 Carson spilled 2 cups of orange juice. Tristan spilled 1 quart of cranberry juice. Who spilled more juice?

7 Maya bought 3 one-quart cans of blue paint and 4 one-pint cans of yellow paint. Did Maya buy more blue or yellow paint?

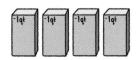

ENGAGE

A tank contains some water. Water from the tank is poured to completely fill some cylinders. Each cylinder has a capacity of 4 quarts. After pouring the water from the tank into the cylinders, 1 quart of water is left. If there are between 15 and 25 quarts of water in the tank at first, what are the greatest and the least number of cylinders used?

LEARN Estimate and measure volume in gallons

1 The **gallon** is another customary unit for measuring volume. gal stands for gallon.

A carton can hold 1 quart of milk.

These 4 cartons hold 4 quarts of milk.
4 quarts of milk can completely fill the container.

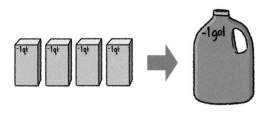

> 1 gallon (gal) = 4 quarts (qt)

The capacity of the container is 1 gallon.

Customary Units of Volume
1 gallon (gal) = 4 quarts (qt)
1 quart = 2 pints (pt)
1 pint = 2 cups (c)
1 cup = 8 fluid ounces (fl oz)

2 A pail holds 8 gallons of water.
   How many pints are there in 8 gallons?

1 gal = 4 qt
1 qt = 2 pt
8 gal = ? pt

TRY Practice estimating and measuring volume in gallons

Choose the best unit for each measure.
Use quart, cup, pint, or gallon.

1 a small carton of milk for

   breakfast _____

2 a large can of paint _____

3 a small carton of orange juice

   _____

4 a medium-sized tomato juice

   container _____

Fill in each blank.

5 3 gal = _____ × _____

   = _____ qt

6 16 gal = _____ × _____

   = _____ qt

   = _____ × _____

   = _____ pt

Compare. Write >, <, or =.

7 8 pt ◯ 1 gal

8 3 gal ◯ 11 qt

9 18 c ◯ 2 gal

Solve.

10 There are 6 gallons of water in a tank. How many pints of water are there?

11 David and his friends drink 5 gallons of milk in a week. How many cups of milk do they drink in a week?

INDEPENDENT PRACTICE

Fill in each blank.

1

The weight of the bunch of

bananas is _____ ounces.

2

The pumpkin weighs

_____ pounds.

Choose the unit you would use to measure the weight of each object. Use ounce, pound, or ton.

3 an egg _____

4 a bus _____

5 a wheelchair _____

6 a bar of chocolate _____

Fill in each blank.

7 32 lb = _____ oz

8 12 T = _____ lb

9 7 T = _____ lb

10 7 qt = _____ pt

11 15 qt = _____ c

12 2 gal = _____ qt

13. 7 gal = _____ pt

14. 6 gal = _____ c

Circle the best estimate.

15. 15 pints / gallons of paint for painting a house

16. 5 cups / quarts of milk for a baby every day

17. 40 gallons / 400 gallons of water in a bathtub

Compare each pair of volumes. Write >, <, or =.

18. 12 T ◯ 20,000 lb

19. 769 oz ◯ 48 lb

20. 60 fl oz ◯ 8 c

21. 3 pt ◯ 48 fl oz

22. 14 qt ◯ 442 fl oz

23. 21 gal ◯ 336 c

Solve.

24. Each carton contains 1 pint of milk.
What is the total amount of milk in the 3 cartons in cups?

25. Amanda spilled 4 cups of water. Victor spilled 1 quart of water.
Who spilled more water?

3 Real-World Problems: Customary Units of Measure

Learning Objective:
• Draw bar models to solve real-world problems involving customary units of measure.

THINK

Caroline took part in a race. In the race, she had to run 1 mile, swim 550 yards, and cycle 4 miles. Find the total distance, in feet, covered by Caroline in the race.

ENGAGE

a The gas tank of Andrea's car can hold 16 gallons of gas. Andrea spent $15 on gas. If she bought 5 gallons of gas, how much did each gallon cost?

b If her car uses 1 gallon of gas for every 26 miles she drives, how far can she travel on a full tank of gas?

LEARN Solve real-world problems involving customary units of measure

1 Luke had an 80-inch piece of wire. He used 4 feet of the wire to make a frame. How many inches of wire did he have left?

STEP 1 Understand the problem.

How long was the piece of wire Luke had at first?
How much of the wire was used?
What do I need to find?

STEP 2 Think of a plan.
I can draw a bar model.

STEP 3 Carry out the plan.

4 feet = 4 × 12
       = 48 in.

80 in.

48 in.   ?

80 − 48 = 32
He had 32 inches of wire left.

STEP 4 Check the answer.
I can work backwards to check my answer.

32 + 48 = 80
My answer is correct.

2 The cost of a pound of blueberries is $4. Thomas bought 6 pounds of blueberries and used 12 ounces to bake a pie.
  a How much did Thomas pay for the blueberries?
  b How many ounces of blueberries did he have left?

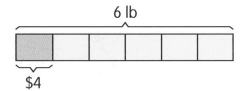

6 lb

$4

a 6 × $4 = $24

Thomas paid $24 for the blueberries.

b 6 lb = 6 × 16
        = 96 oz

  96 − 12 = 84

He had 84 ounces of blueberries left.

Hands-on Activity Creating and solving real-world problems involving customary units of measure

Work in groups.

(1) Complete each story using the words and numbers provided.

32	2	8	yellow
1	1,050	blue	1,810

a Gavin buys 2 pounds of strawberries.
   He packs them equally into 4 containers.

   The total weight of the strawberries is _____ ounces.

   Each container weighs _____ ounces.

b Ashley bought 3 one-quart cans of blue paint and 4 one-pint cans of yellow paint.

   She bought _____ quart(s) more _____ paint

   than _____ paint.

c Felipe jogged 1 mile.
   He then took a short-cut and walked 50 yards home.
   The distance that Felipe jogged and walked altogether

   was _____ yards.

3 David made 2 gallons of fruit punch. He poured the punch equally into 6 glasses.
   a How much punch was there in each glass in fluid ounces?
   b How much punch was left over?

4 A family of elephants lives in a zoo. The female adult elephant gives birth to 2 baby elephants weighing 220 pounds each. The adult male elephant weighs 6 tons and the adult female elephant weighs 4 tons. Find the total weight of the family of elephants in pounds.

4 Length in Metric Units

Learning Objectives:
- Measure and estimate lengths in metric units.
- Convert between different units of measurement of length.

New Vocabulary
kilometer (km)

THINK

Briella cycles to school and back home everyday. The distance between her school and her home is 3 kilometers. How far does she travel in meters in a week?

ENGAGE

Lily has just learned how to measure length in centimeters. She is asked to measure the width of a basketball court in centimeters. How can Lily measure the width of the basketball court? What is another way to measure the length?

LEARN Measure length in meters and centimeters

1 The guitar is 1 meter long.

> 1 meter is 100 times as long as 1 centimeter.
> 1 m = 100 cm

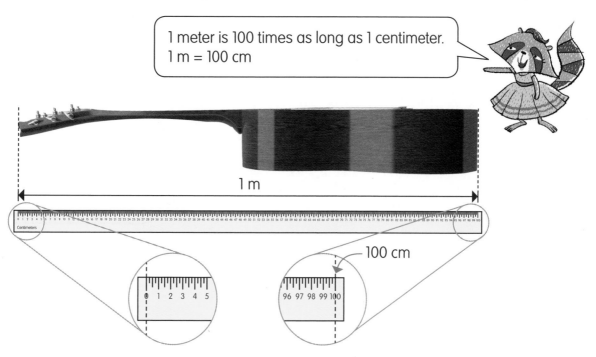

2 The mop is 1 meter 57 centimeters long.
Find the length of the mop in centimeters.

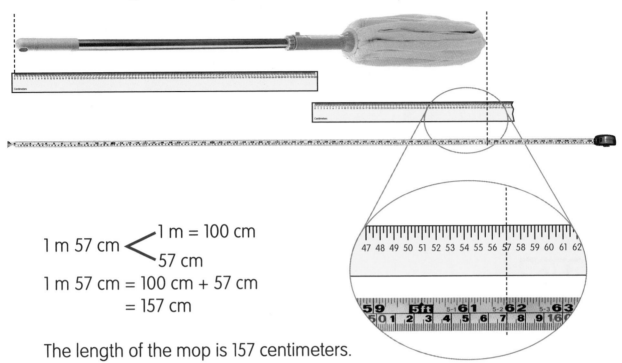

1 m 57 cm $\begin{cases} 1\text{ m} = 100\text{ cm} \\ 57\text{ cm} \end{cases}$

1 m 57 cm = 100 cm + 57 cm
= 157 cm

The length of the mop is 157 centimeters.

3 Kylie jumped 125 centimeters from the starting line.
How far did she jump in meters and centimeters?

125 cm $\begin{cases} 100\text{ cm} = 1\text{ m} \\ 25\text{ cm} \end{cases}$

125 cm = 100 cm + 25 cm
= 1 m 25 cm

Kylie jumped 1 meter 25 centimeters.

Work in pairs.

1. Stay behind a line. Place a meter rule next to the line. Throw a bean bag as far as you can.

2. Estimate how far the bean bag is from the line.

		My Estimate	My Measure
Distance from starting line	Try 1	_____ m _____ cm	_____ m _____ cm
	Try 2		

3. Measure the distance with a meter rule.

4. Remove the meter rule and throw the bean bag again. Estimate if the throw is farther this time.

TRY Practice measuring length in meters and centimeters

Write each length in centimeters.

1. 4 m 56 cm

   = _____ cm + _____ cm

   = _____ cm

2. 8 m 32 cm

   = _____ cm + _____ cm

   = _____ cm

4 m = 4 × 100 cm

Write each length in meters and centimeters.

3 270 cm = _____ cm + _____ cm

= _____ m _____ cm

4 306 cm = _____ m _____ cm

Compare each pair of lengths. Write >, <, or =.

5 25 cm ◯ 5 m

6 790 cm ◯ 7 m

ENGAGE

a A running track is 400 meters long. Kaitlyn runs around the track three times. How many meters does she run in all? Draw a diagram to show your thinking.

b Show three different ways you can use to represent the total distance Kaitlyn ran. Which is the most convenient way?

LEARN Measure length and distance in kilometers and meters

1 A train is about 1,000 meters long. It is about 1 kilometer.

The kilometer (km) is also a unit of length.

1 km = 1,000 m

2

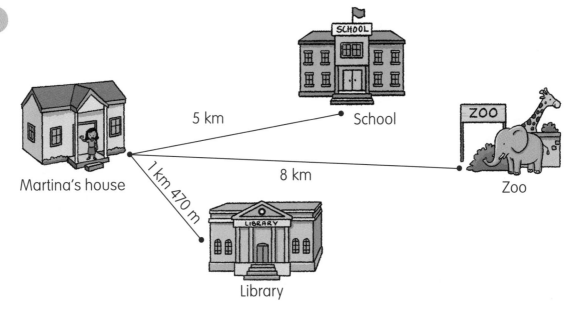

Martina's house   5 km   School

1 km 470 m

8 km   Zoo

Library

The school is 5 kilometers from Martina's house.
The zoo is 8 kilometers from Martina's house.

The distance between the library and Martina's house is 1 kilometer
470 meters. What is the distance in meters?

1 km 470 m $\begin{cases} \text{1 km = 1,000 m} \\ \text{470 m} \end{cases}$

1 km 470 m = 1,000 m + 470 m
= 1,470 m

The distance is 1,470 meters.

3 A plane flies 2,790 meters above the ground.
How high is the plane above the ground?
Express the answer in kilometers and meters.

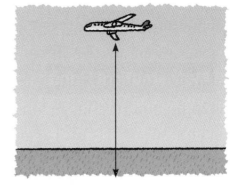

2,790 m $\begin{cases} \text{2,000 m = 2 km} \\ \text{790 m} \end{cases}$

2,790 m = 2 km + 790 m
= 2 km 790 m

The plane is 2 kilometers 790 meters above the ground.

TRY Practice measuring length and distance in kilometers and meters

Write the length in meters.

1 4 km 235 m = _____ m + _____ m

= _____ m

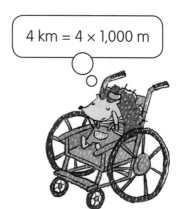

4 km = 4 × 1,000 m

Write the length in kilometers and meters.

2 6,042 m = _____ m + _____ m

= _____ km _____ m

Fill in the blank.

3 Ariana and Elijah cycled around a park. The distance that Ariana cycled was 2 kilometers 350 meters. The distance that Elijah cycled was 2,375 meters. Who cycled a greater distance?

2 km 350 m = 2,000 m + 350 m
= 2,350 m

2,350 m < 2,375 m

_____ cycled a greater distance.

MATH SHARING

Mathematical Habit 5 Use tools strategically

Name a place that you think is 1 kilometer away from your school.
How can you check if your guess is correct?
Share your ideas with your classmates.

© 2020 Marshall Cavendish Education Pte Ltd

INDEPENDENT PRACTICE

Write each length in centimeters, or meters and centimeters.

1 6 m 8 cm = _____ cm

2 137 cm = _____ m _____ cm

Write each length in meters, or kilometers and meters.

3 5 km 97 m = _____ m

4 4,162 m = _____ km _____ m

Fill in each blank.

5 5 m 81 cm = _____ cm

6 204 cm = _____ m _____ cm

7 8,050 m = _____ km _____ m

8 9 km 2 m = _____ m

Compare each pair of lengths. Write >, <, or =.

9 63 cm $\bigcirc$ 6 m 3 cm

10 531 m $\bigcirc$ 5 km 310 m

11 2,062 m $\bigcirc$ 2 km 62 m

12 7 km 269 m $\bigcirc$ 7,029 m

Solve.

13 Katherine jogged 2 kilometers and 860 meters on a Saturday.
Silas jogged 2,086 meters on the same Saturday.
Who jogged a longer distance?

14 Justin walked 670 meters to the park every day.
What is the total distance walked in 5 days in kilometres and meters?

5 Mass and Volume in Metric Units

Learning Objective:
- Convert between different units of measurement of mass and volume.

THINK

The mass of a 20-liter pail completely filled with paint was 24,392 grams. After 8,215 milliliters of paint were used, the mass of the pail decreased to 14 kilograms 559 grams.

a What was the mass of the paint that was used?
b How many milliliters of paint were left?

ENGAGE

A 1-liter filled water bottle, a pineapple, and a small watermelon are things that have a mass of about 1 kilogram each. Belle said that the total mass of the three items was more than 3 kilograms. Do you agree with Belle? Explain using examples.

LEARN Measure mass in kilograms and grams

1 A luggage has a mass of 5 kilograms 678 grams.
What is the mass of the luggage in grams?

$$5 \text{ kg } 678 \text{ g} \begin{cases} 5 \text{ kg} = 5,000 \text{ g} \\ 678 \text{ g} \end{cases}$$

1 kg = 1,000 g

5 kg 678 g = 5,000 g + 678 g
= 5,678 g

The mass of the luggage is 5,678 grams.

2 The mass of a box of books is 12,865 grams. What is its mass in kilograms and grams?

$$12,865 \text{ g} \begin{cases} 12,000 \text{ g} = 12 \text{ kg} \\ 865 \text{ g} \end{cases}$$

12,865 g = 12,000 g + 865 g
      = 12 kg 865 g

The mass of the box of books is 12 kilograms 865 grams.

TRY Practice measuring mass in kilograms and grams

Write each mass in kilograms and grams.

1 15,805 g = _____ g + _____ g

= _____ kg _____ g

2 18,794 g = _____ g + _____ g

= _____ kg _____ g

Write each mass in grams.

3 16 kg 522 g = _____ g + _____ g

= _____ g

4 29 kg 473 g = _____ g + _____ g

= _____ g

Compare each pair of masses. Write >, <, or =.

5 31 kg 4 g ◯ 31,400 g

6 72,468 g ◯ 72 kg 468 g

ENGAGE

Anna completely fills a bottle with water. She pours all the water from it into 3 identical containers of volume 400 milliliters each and half of a container of volume 400 milliliters. Explain how you find the capacity of the bottle.

LEARN Measure volume in liters and milliliters

1. The volume of water in a pail is 3 liters 126 milliliters.
   What is the volume in milliliters?

   1 L = 1,000 mL

   3 L 126 mL $\Big\langle$ 3 L = 3000 mL
   126 mL

   3 L 126 mL = 3,000 mL + 126 mL
   = 3,126 mL

   The volume of water is 3,126 milliliters.

2. The capacity of a barrel is 18,927 milliliters.
   What is the capacity of the barrel in liters and milliliters?

   18,927 mL $\Big\langle$ 18,000 mL = 18 L
   927 mL

   18,927 mL = 18,000 mL + 927 mL
   = 18 L 927 mL

   The barrel has a capacity of 18 liters 927 milliliters.

TRY Practice measuring volume in liters and milliliters

Write each volume in milliliters.

1. 2 L 725 mL = _____ mL + _____ mL

   = _____ mL

2. 14 L 803 mL = _____ mL + _____ mL

   = _____ mL

Write each volume in liters and milliliters.

3. 6,892 mL = _____ mL + _____ mL

   = _____ L _____ mL

4. 11,427 = _____ mL + _____ mL

   = _____ L _____ mL

Compare each pair of volumes. Write >, <, or =.

5. 3,250 mL $\bigcirc$ 3 L

6. 15 L $\bigcirc$ 15,020 mL

7. 56 L 2 mL $\bigcirc$ 56,002 mL

8. 46,086 mL $\bigcirc$ 46 L 860 mL

INDEPENDENT PRACTICE

Write each mass in grams.

1. 19 kg 398 g = _____ g

2. 72 kg 541 g = _____ g

Write each mass in kilograms and grams.

3. 46,847 g = _____ kg + _____ g

4. 58,962 g = _____ kg + _____ g

Write each volume in milliliters.

5. 15 L 249 mL = _____ mL

6. 81 L 123 mL = _____ mL

Write each volume in liters and milliliters.

7. 30,027 mL = _____ L + _____ mL

8. 79,064 mL = _____ L + _____ mL

Compare each pair of masses. Write >, <, or =.

9 23 kg 3 g $\bigcirc$ 23,300 g

10 36,089 g $\bigcirc$ 36 kg 89 g

Compare each pair of volumes. Write >, <, or =.

11 17,274 mL $\bigcirc$ 17 L 247 mL

12 43 L 916 mL $\bigcirc$ 43,196 mL

Compare each pair of volumes. Write >, <, or =.

13 The capacity of a pail is 13 liters 500 milliliters. The volume of water in the pail is 6,324 milliliters. How much more water is needed to fill the pail completely? Give your answer in milliliters.

14 A monkey weighs 5,364 grams. An antelope weighs 19 kilograms 968 grams. What is the total mass of the monkey and the antelope? Give your answer in kilograms and grams.

6 Real-World Problems: Metric Units of Measure

Learning Objective:
- Draw bar models to solve real-world problems involving metric units of measure.

 THINK

Ryan participated in a triathlon where he had to swim 1.5 kilometers, cycle 20 times the distance he had swum, and run $\frac{1}{3}$ of the distance he had cycled.

What was the total distance he had covered, and convert it into meters?

ENGAGE

A box of cereal has a weight of 480 grams. A pack of crackers has a weight of 340 grams. What is the total weight of 3 boxes of cereal and 2 packs of crackers?
Discuss two different strategies to find the answer. Does each strategy give the same answer? Explain.

LEARN Solve real-world problems involving metric units of measure

1) Aubrey walked 650 meters from her school to the shopping mall. On her way back to school, she walked to the train station to meet her friend. She walked from the train station back to her school. What was the total distance she walked? Give your answer in kilometers and meters.

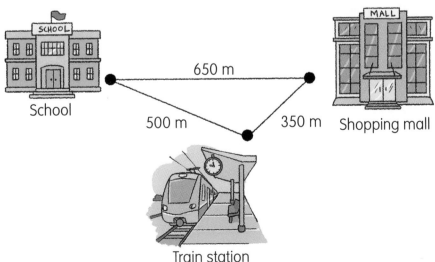

School   650 m   Shopping mall
500 m   350 m
Train station

STEP 1 Understand the problem.

How far is Aubrey's school from the shopping mall?
How far is the train station from the shopping mall?
How far is the train station from her school?
What do I need to find?

STEP 2 Think of a plan.
I can draw a bar model.

STEP 3 Carry out the plan.

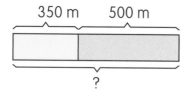

350 m   500 m

?

350 + 500 = 850

The distance from the shopping mall to the train station and back to the school was 850 meters.

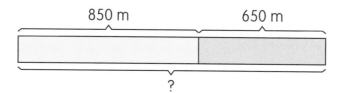

850 m   650 m

?

850 + 650 = 1,500

1,500 m = 1,000 m + 500 m
= 1 km 500 m

STEP 4 Check the answer.
I can work backwards to check my answers.

> 1 km 500 m = 1,000 m + 500 m
>   = 1,500 m
>
> 1,500 − 650 = 850
>   850 − 500 = 350
>
> My answer is correct.

2 Natalie had 9 containers.
Each container contained 3 liters of water.
She wanted to fill a tank with a capacity of 35 liters.
How many more liters of water did she need to completely fill the tank?

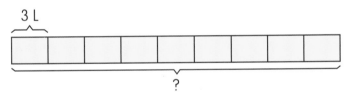

$9 \times 3 = 27$
9 containers contained 27 liters of water.

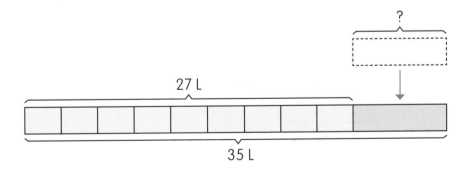

$35 − 27 = 8$

Natalie needed 8 more liters of water to completely fill the tank.

TRY Practice solving real-world problems involving metric units of measure

Solve.

1 Adriana and Samuel were in a race.
   Each of them cycled from Point A to Point B and ran from Point B to Point C.

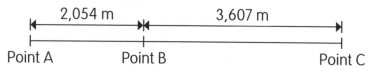

| 2,054 m | 3,607 m |

Point A   Point B   Point C

When Adriana finished the race, Samuel had only completed 1,036 m.
How much farther did Samuel have to complete to finish the race?
Give your answer in kilometers and meters.

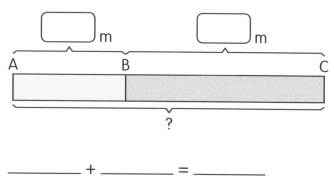

_____ + _____ = _____

The distance of the whole race was _____ meters.

First, find the distance of the whole race.

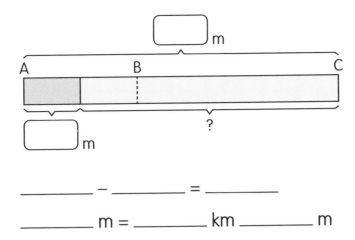

_____ − _____ = _____

_____ m = _____ km _____ m

Samuel had to complete another _____ kilometers _____ meters to finish the race.

2 A store sold kidney beans in bags of 2 kilograms at $7 each. Henry bought 8 bags and paid using a $100 bill.
  a How many kilograms of beans did he buy?
  b How much change did he receive?

a _____ ◯ _____ = _____

He bought _____ kilograms of kidney beans.

b $_____ ◯ _____ = $_____

$_____ − $_____ = $_____

He received $_____ change.

INDEPENDENT PRACTICE

Solve. Draw a bar model to help you.

1 Kiara, Mariah, Abigail, and Jade ran in a 1-kilometer charity relay race. Kiara ran $\frac{1}{4}$ kilometer, Mariah ran $\frac{3}{8}$ kilometer, and Jade ran $\frac{1}{8}$ kilometer. What fraction of the race did Abigail run?

Solve.

2 Sean jogged 1,802 meters to the park. He then took a short cut and walked 912 meters home. What is the distance Sean jogged and walked altogether in kilometers and meters?

3. A bag of onions has a mass of 550 grams. A bag of garlic has a mass of 800 grams. Katelyn bought 5 bags of onions and 4 bags of garlic. What is the total mass of onions and garlic that Katelyn bought in kilograms and grams?

4. William used 950 milliliters of water and 550 milliliters of lemon juice to make lemonade. He poured the lemonade into 4 glasses. How many milliliters of lemonade were poured into each glass?

5 A bottle contained 800 milliliters of juice. A carton contained 12 such bottles. Each carton of juice cost $24. A restaurant bought 12 cartons of the juice.
   a How many liters and milliliters of juice did the restaurant buy in total?
   b How much did the restaurant pay for the juice in total?

7 Time

Learning Objectives:
- Measure time in seconds.
- Convert units of time.
- Read and tell time using the 24-hour clock.
- Solve real-world problems involving time.

THINK

The time shown on a clock is 10 o'clock. After a period of more than 1 hour but less than 3 hours, the minute hand on the clock is pointing at 9. What are the possible times? How do you write the time in 24-hour clock?

ENGAGE

Record the time taken for each person from your group to write their names 30 times. Discuss different ways to tell the times recorded.

LEARN Convert units of time

1 The second is a unit of measurement for time.
s stands for seconds.

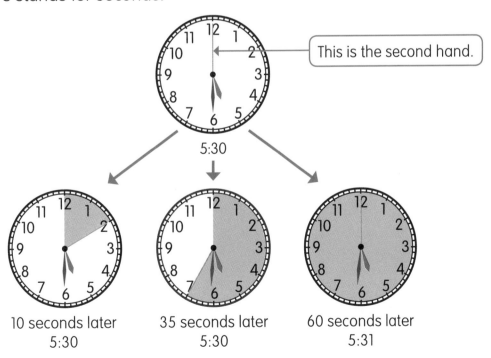

This is the second hand.

5:30

10 seconds later
5:30

35 seconds later
5:30

60 seconds later
5:31

60 seconds (s) = 1 minute (min)

2 Miguel walks from one end of a classroom to the other. Mr. Williams times him.

5 s later

5 s later

Miguel takes 10 seconds to walk from one end of the classroom to the other.

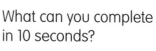

What can you complete in 10 seconds?

3 What is 2 minutes in seconds?

1 min = 60 s
2 min = 2 × 60
     = 120 s

2 minutes is 120 seconds.

4 Express 5 minutes 45 seconds in seconds.

5 min = 5 × 60
     = 300 s

5 min 45 s = 300 + 45
        = 345 s

5 minutes 45 seconds is 345 seconds.

Hands-on Activity Identify activities that can be done in 1 second

Work in pairs.

① Estimate whether each activity in the table would take 1 second, more than 1 second, or less than 1 second.

Activity	1 s	More than 1 s	Less than 1 s	Actual time
Say "thirty-four"				
Blink once				
Raise your hand				
Nod twice				
Say your full name				

② Ask your partner to measure the time you take to complete each activity. Then, record your time in the table.

③ Trade places. Repeat ① and ②.

TRY Practice converting time

Fill in each blank.

① What is 4 minutes in seconds?

1 min = _____ s

4 min = _____ × _____

= _____ s

4 minutes is _____ seconds.

② Express 2 minutes 18 seconds in seconds.

2 min = _____ × _____   2 min 18 s = _____ + _____

= _____ s   = _____ s

2 minutes 18 seconds is _____ seconds.

ENGAGE

The clock shows half past 12 in the afternoon. What is the time shown on the clock 80 minutes later? What is another way to show the time? Share your ideas with your partner.

LEARN Read and tell time using the 24-hour clock

1

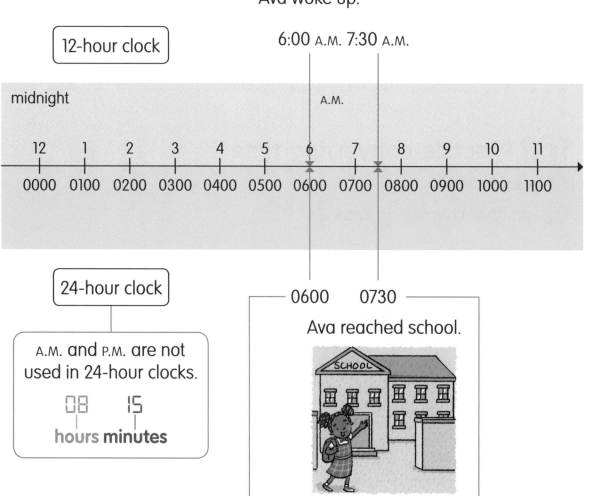

Ava woke up.

6:00 A.M. 7:30 A.M.

12-hour clock

midnight   A.M.

12   1   2   3   4   5   6   7   8   9   10   11

0000 0100 0200 0300 0400 0500 0600 0700 0800 0900 1000 1100

24-hour clock

0600   0730

Ava reached school.

A.M. and P.M. are not used in 24-hour clocks.

08   15
hours minutes

Read as zero six hundred hours.

Read as zero seven thirty hours.

Ava went home.

Ava had dinner.

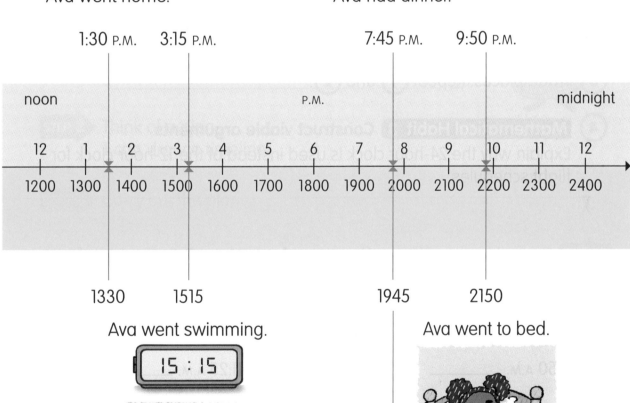

1:30 P.M.   3:15 P.M.   7:45 P.M.   9:50 P.M.

| noon | | | | | | P.M. | | | | | midnight |

| 12 | 1 | 2 | 3 | 4 | 5 | 6 | 7 | 8 | 9 | 10 | 11 | 12 |
| 1200 | 1300 | 1400 | 1500 | 1600 | 1700 | 1800 | 1900 | 2000 | 2100 | 2200 | 2300 | 2400 |

1330   1515   1945   2150

Ava went swimming.   Ava went to bed.

15 : 15

Read as nineteen forty-five hours.

2 A plane left Airport J at 1345 and arrived at Airport K at 1510 on the same day. How long was the journey in hours and minutes?

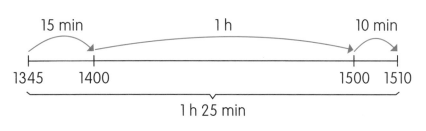

Draw a timeline to show the time taken.

The journey was 1 hour 25 minutes long.

3 Michael watched a movie that lasted 2 hours 30 minutes. The movie ended at 1500. What time did the movie start?

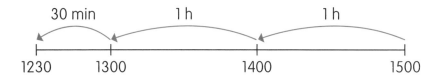

The movie started at 1230.

4 Ms. Lewis went to a concert on Saturday. The concert ended at 2330. She reached home 45 minutes later. What time did she reach home?

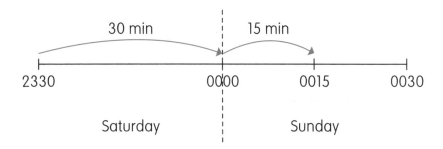

Ms. Lewis reached home at 0015 on Sunday.

5   David's art lesson started at 1530. The lesson lasted 1 hour 10 minutes. What time did the art lesson end?

▶ **Method 1**

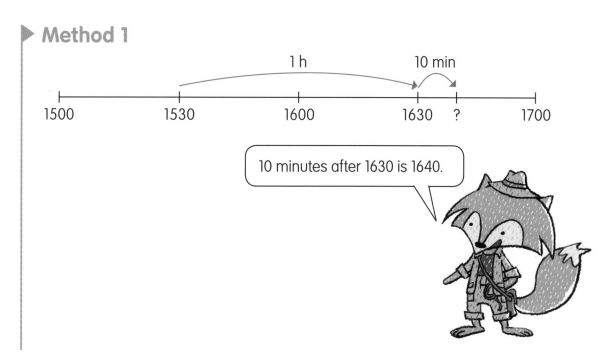

10 minutes after 1630 is 1640.

▶ **Method 2**

1 h 10 min = 70 min
        = 30 min + 40 min

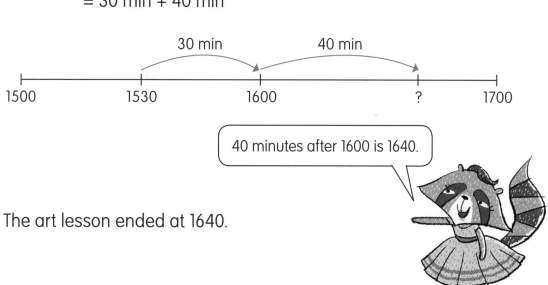

40 minutes after 1600 is 1640.

The art lesson ended at 1640.

Hands-on Activity — Creating real-world problems involving the 24-hour clock

Work in groups.

① Use the following to create a word problem.

2034	1 h 45 min	Eugene	homework
begin	finished	what time	he took

② Exchange problem with another group.

③ Solve the problem using a timeline.

TRY Practice solving real-world problems involving time

Solve. Use the timeline to help you.

1 A plane departed City Y at 2250 on Wednesday. It landed in City Z at 0120. How long was the flight in hours and minutes? Did the plane reach City Z on the same day or the next day?

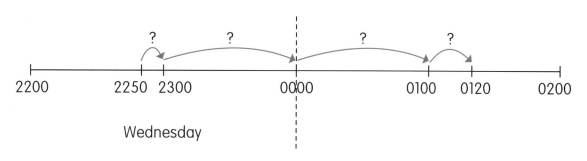

Wednesday

From	To	Time Taken
2250	2300	
2300	0000	
0000	0100	
0100	0120	

The flight was _____ hours _____ minutes long.

The plane reached City Z on the _____ day.

2 A movie ended at 2205. It lasted 2 hours 25 minutes.
What time did the movie start?

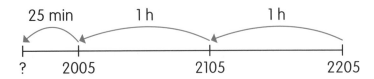

The movie started at _____.

3 Brooklyn took the train at Station P and reached Station Q 26 minutes later.
She arrived at Station Q at 1120.
What time did Brooklyn board the train at Station P?

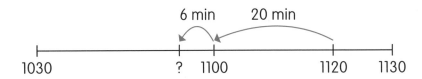

Brooklyn boarded the train at _____.

Mathematical Habit 6 Use precise mathematical language
Using the 24-hour clock, make a list of your activities on a school day from the time you wake up to the time you go to bed.

© 2020 Marshall Cavendish Education Pte Ltd

INDEPENDENT PRACTICE

Write each time in seconds or minutes.

1 4 min = _____ s

2 12 min = _____ s

3 3 min 51 s = _____ s

Write each time using the 24-hour clock.

4 10:35 A.M.

_____

5 7:50 P.M.

_____

Write each time using the 12-hour clock.

6 0430

_____

7 2305

_____

Solve. Draw a timeline to help you.

8 Alexis slept at 2255 on Saturday. She woke up at 0830 on Sunday. How long did Alexis sleep in hours and minutes?

9 Nicole started her piano lesson at 0930. The lesson lasted 45 minutes. What time did her lesson end?

10 A musical was 2 hours 15 minutes long. It ended at 2245. What time did the musical start?

MATH JOURNAL

Mathematical Habit 3 **Construct viable arguments**

Look at the following conversions. Which is correct? Explain.

(A) 2 gal = 10 pt

(B) 3 lb = 48 oz

(C) 5 yd = 8 ft

(D) 12 km = 120 m

(E) 3 L = 3,000 mL

1 **Mathematical Habit 4** Use mathematical models

Michelle spent 1 hour 20 minutes doing her homework. Then, she spent 20 minutes doing chores and feeding her goldfish. Finally, she practiced the saxophone for 35 minutes until 2100.
What time did she begin doing her homework?

Use the timeline to help you.

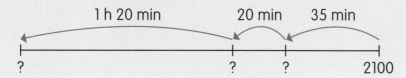

© 2020 Marshall Cavendish Education Pte Ltd

2 **Mathematical Habit 8** Look for patterns

Tyler has a 12-liter pail and a 5-liter pail.
Explain how he can get the following amount of water using these pails.

a   2 liters

b   3 liters

CHAPTER WRAP-UP

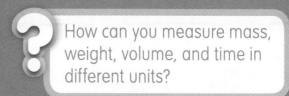

How can you measure mass, weight, volume, and time in different units?

Conversion of Measurements

Length

Use a ruler or measuring tape to find length.

Conversion

Convert measurements of length:

1 mi = 1,760 yd
1 yd = 3 ft
1 ft = 12 in.

1 km = 1,000 m
1 m = 100 cm

Weight and Mass

Use a weighing scale to find mass.

Conversion

Convert measurements of mass:

1 T = 2,000 lb
1 lb = 16 oz

1 kg = 1,000 g

Volume

Volume is the amount of liquid in a container.

Capacity is the amount of liquid a container can hold.

Use measuring cups to find volume.

Conversion

Convert measurements of volume:

1 gal = 4 qt
1 qt = 2 pt
1 pt = 2 c
1 c = 8 fl oz

1 L = 1,000 mL

Time

Measure time in seconds (s).

Use the 24-hour clock.
1 A.M. is 0100 hours.
1 P.M. is 1300 hours.

Conversion

Convert measurement of time:

1 h = 60 min
1 min = 60 s

Solve real-world problems

Name: _____ Date: _____

Fill in each blank.

1 6 ft = _____ in.

2 34 yd = _____ ft

3 9 mi = _____ yd

4 15 yd = _____ in.

5 46 lb = _____ oz

6 24 T = _____ lb

7 56 gal = _____ qt

8 74 qt = _____ c

9 126 pt = _____ fl oz

Compare each pair of measurements. Write >, <, or =.

10 829 in. ◯ 23 yd

11 3 mi ◯ 15,840 ft

12 17 lb ◯ 270 oz

13 34,140 lb ◯ 18 T

14 473 fl oz ◯ 30 pt

15 39 qt ◯ 156 c

16 16 gal ◯ 2,050 fl oz

Solve.

17 A bottle is filled with 2 quarts of drink. A box contained 18 such bottles. A restaurant sold the drink by cups, with each cup of drink for $6.

   a How many cups of drinks did the restaurant sell in all?

   b How much money did the restaurant collect if all the cups of drink are sold?

18 James ran $2\frac{1}{2}$ miles a day for 4 days in a park. He walked 983 yards a day for another 5 days. What is the total distance James ran and walked in yards?

19 The weight of a bag of black beans was 12 pounds. The weight of a bag of green beans was 214 ounces. The beans were mixed and packed into 6 bags.

a What is the weight of the mixed beans in each bag in ounces?

b What was the weight of the beans that were not packed?

Fill in each blank.

20 7 m 69 cm = _____ cm

21 641 cm = _____ m _____ cm

22 8,905 m = _____ km _____ m

23 43 km 509 m = _____ m

24 54 kg 375 g = _____ g

25 38,555 g = _____ kg _____ g

26 39 L 948 mL = _____ mL

27 60,924 mL = _____ L _____ mL

28 9 min 59 s = _____ s

29 1 h 38 min = _____ s

Write each time using the 24-hour clock.

30 09:59 A.M.

_____

31 6:03 P.M.

_____

Write each time using the 12-hour clock.

32 2147

_____

33 0001

_____

Compare each pair of measurements. Write >, <, or =.

34 2 m 9 cm ◯ 29 cm

35 6,014 m ◯ 6 km 14 m

36 8 km 241 m ◯ 8,024 m

37 730 cm ◯ 73 m

38 45 kg 6 g ◯ 45,600 g

39 23,024 g ◯ 23 kg 24 g

40 37,001 mL ◯ 37 L 10 mL

41 80 L 11 mL ◯ 80,011 mL

Solve. Draw a timeline to help you.

42 A man drove from Town A to Town B for 2 hours 26 minutes. He was in Town B for 45 minutes. Then, he returned from Town B to Town A in 1 hour 12 minutes. He left Town A at 8 A.M. At what time did he return to Town A?

Solve. Draw bar models to help you.

43 A bag containing 5 apples has a mass of 1 kilogram 200 grams. The mass of the empty box is 360 grams. What is the mass of each apple if the apples have the same mass?

44 A street has 16 street lamps at an equal distance from one another. Each pair of street lamps is 460 meters apart. How long is the street? Give your answers in kilometers and meters.

45 Vanessa filled a bottle completely with water for her rabbit. Her rabbit drank 250 milliliters of water a day. After a week, the bottle was empty.
   a How much water was in the bottle at first?

   b Vanessa filled the bottle completely again. She spilled some water, leaving 1 liter of water in the bottle. How many milliliters of water did she spill?

Assessment Prep

Answer each question.

46 What is 7 kilometers 429 meters in meters?

   Ⓐ 749 m

   Ⓑ 7,029 m

   Ⓒ 7,429 m

   Ⓓ 7,940 m

47 What is 24 pounds in ounces?

   Ⓐ 8 oz

   Ⓑ 40 oz

   Ⓒ 48 oz

   Ⓓ 384 oz

48 What is 2 hours 9 minutes in seconds?

   Ⓐ 129 s

   Ⓑ 660 s

   Ⓒ 7,209 s

   Ⓓ 7,740 s

Name: _____ Date: _____

Clues on the Board

1 Ms. Taylor, Ms. Johnson, and Mr. Davis made an "All About Me" poster in the hallway of Exley Elementary School to show facts about themselves. However, they did not include their names.

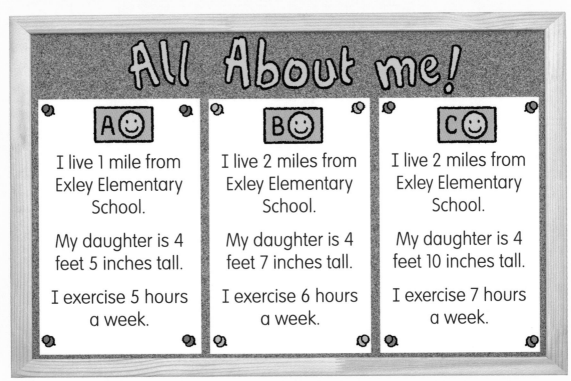

Convert each distance into feet, each height into inches, and each time into minutes. Then, match the posters to the clues.

Poster A:

Poster B:

Poster C:

They gave the following clues so that students could determine which information belongs to whom.

Ms. Taylor
Clue 1: I exercise 420 minutes a week.
Clue 2: I live 10,560 feet from Exley Elementary School.
Clue 3: My daughter is 58 inches tall.

Ms. Johnson
Clue 1: I live 10,560 feet from Exley Elementary School.
Clue 2: I exercise 360 minutes a week.
Clue 3: My daughter is 55 inches tall.

Mr. Davis
Clue 1: My daughter is 53 inches tall.
Clue 2: I live 5,280 feet from Exley Elementary School.
Clue 3: I exercise 300 minutes a week.

Use the clues to figure out who made each poster.
Show your work.

Poster A: _____

Poster B: _____

Poster C: _____

2 Mr. Davis and Ms. Johnson practiced running for the 5-kilometer fun run. Each morning, Mr. Davis ran 3 kilometers through the park by the school, while Ms. Johnson ran 7 laps round the school's track. Each lap that Ms. Johnson ran was 400 meters. Who ran a longer distance each morning? Show your work.

3 After the fun run, Mr. Davis drank 5 cups of water and Ms. Johnson drank 3 pints of water. Who drank more water after the run? Explain your work.

Rubric

Point(s)	Level	My Performance
7–8	4	• Most of my answers are correct. • I showed complete understanding of what I have learned. • I used the correct strategies to solve the problems. • I explained my answers and mathematical thinking clearly and completely.
5–6	3	• Some of my answers are correct. • I showed some understanding of what I have learned. • I used some correct strategies to solve the problems. • I explained my answers and mathematical thinking clearly.
3–4	2	• A few of my answers are correct. • I showed little understanding of what I have learned. • I used a few correct strategies to solve the problems. • I explained some of my answers and mathematical thinking clearly.
0–2	1	• A few of my answers are correct. • I showed little or no understanding of what I have learned. • I used a few strategies to solve the problems. • I did not explain my answers and mathematical thinking clearly.

Teacher's Comments

STEAM

Amazing Tongues

Have you ever noticed the tiny bumps on the surface of your tongue? There are about 10,000 of them, and they contain taste buds.

Your tongue does more than help you chew and taste food. It also helps you make the sounds you use to speak.

Other living things also have useful tongues. They use their tongues to eat and chew, and even to make sounds, like you do. But some also use their tongues to clean their skin and fur, gather information, and capture prey.

Task

Compare Tongues

Work in pairs to learn about animal tongues.

1. Make a list of questions about tongues. For example: What animal has the longest tongue? What does the animal use its tongue to do? What shape is it? What color is it? Does it have any special features, such as spines or hooks?

2. Use a library or the internet to find answers to your questions. Look for books like *Animal Tongues* by Dawn Cusick. Or visit online sites of places such as the San Diego Zoo.

3. Record measurements and take notes. Use paper and other art supplies or software to display the information you gather. Include a drawing of each animal's tongue. Draw each tongue to its actual length. Label the measurement in both inches and centimeters.

4. Display the drawings on a class wall, in the order of the tongue's length, from the shortest to the longest.

Area and Perimeter

What is the area occupied by the Art Exhibition?

How do you find the perimeter and area of a rectangle or square using a formula? How do you find an unknown side of a rectangle or square, given its area or perimeter?

RECALL PRIOR KNOWLEDGE

Understanding and finding the perimeter of a figure

The perimeter of a figure is the distance around it.

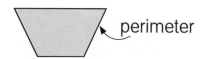 perimeter

The standard units used for shorter distances are centimeter (cm) and inch (in.). The standard units used for longer distances are meter (m) and foot (ft).

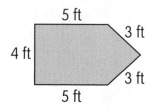

You can add the lengths of sides to find the perimeter.
Perimeter = 5 + 3 + 3 + 5 + 4
           = 20 ft

The perimeter of the figure is 20 feet.

▶ Quick Check

Find the perimeter of each figure.

1

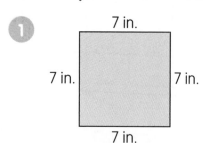

2

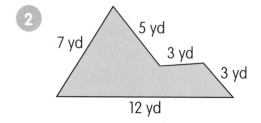

Finding an unknown side given the perimeter

The perimeter of Figure *ABCDE* is 32 inches. Find the length of *CD*.

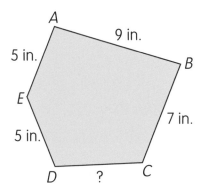

Perimeter = 32 in.

$9 + 7 + CD + 5 + 5 = 32$

$26 + CD = 32$

$CD = 32 - 26$

$= 6$ in.

The length of *CD* is 6 inches.

▶ **Quick Check**

Find the length of the unknown side.

3 The perimeter of the rectangle is 40 centimeters. Find the length of the unknown side.

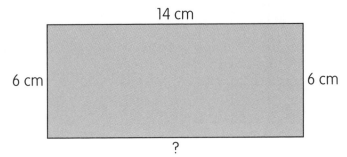

Understanding and finding area of a figure

The area of a figure is the amount of surface covered by the figure.

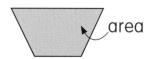area

The standard units used for small areas are square centimeter (cm^2) and square inch (in^2). The standard units used for large areas are square meter (m^2) and square foot (ft^2).

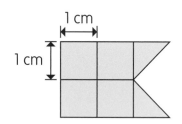

You can count square units to find the area.
The figure is made up of 4 one-centimeter squares and 2 half-squares.
The area of the figure is 5 square centimeters.

▶ Quick Check

Count the square units to find the area of each figure.
The figures are not drawn to scale.

4

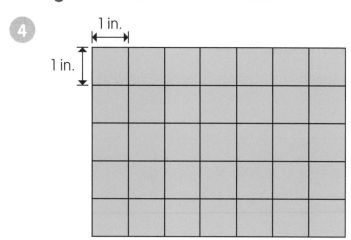

5

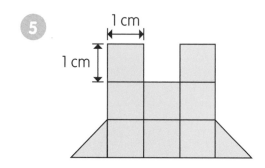

Finding the area of a square or rectangle by multiplying its side lengths

You can find the area of a rectangle or square by multiplying its side lengths.

Area of the rectangle = 7 × 4
= 28 cm^2

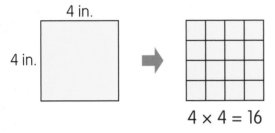

Area of the square = 4 × 4
= 16 in^2

▶ **Quick Check**

Find the area of the rectangle.

6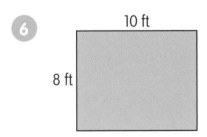

Find the area of the square.

7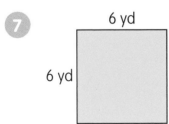

Finding area of a figure by separating it into rectangles

You can find the area of a figure by adding the areas of each shape it is made up of.

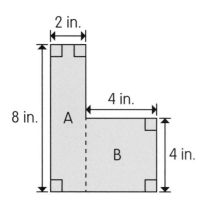

Area of Rectangle A = 8 × 2
= 16 in²
Area of Square B = 4 × 4
= 16 in²
Area of the figure = 16 + 16
= 32 in²

The area of the figure is 32 square inches.

▶ Quick Check

**Draw lines to separate each figure into rectangles.
Find the area of the figure.**

8

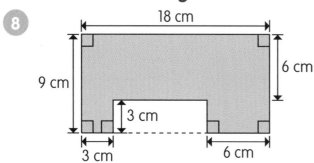

Area and Unknown Sides

Learning Objectives:
- Find the perimeter and area of a rectangle or square using a formula.
- Find the unknown side of a rectangle or square given its perimeter and one known side.
- Find the unknown side of a rectangle or square given its area and one known side.

> **New Vocabulary**
> formula

 **THINK**

Daniel has a square piece of paper. The side lengths of the square are whole numbers. He cuts out a smaller square with an area of 16 square centimeters from the paper. What is the least possible area of

a the square piece of paper at first?
b the remaining piece of paper?

ENGAGE

How can you find the perimeter of the figure? How did the sides you know help you to find the sides you do not know? Explain.

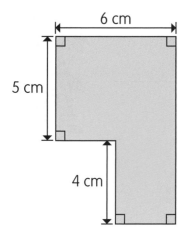

LEARN Find the perimeter of a rectangle or square using a formula

1 The length of a rectangle is 4 inches. The width of the rectangle is 3 inches. Find the perimeter of the rectangle.

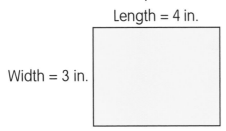

Length = 4 in.

Width = 3 in.

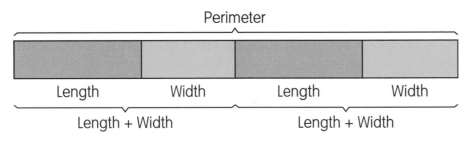

Perimeter

| Length | Width | Length | Width |

Length + Width   Length + Width

The model below shows that the perimeter of the rectangle is the sum of its two lengths and two widths.

You can use a **formula** to find the perimeter of the rectangle.

Perimeter of a rectangle
= (2 × Length) + (2 × Width)
= 2 × (Length + Width)

A formula is a mathematical rule that shows the relationship between two or more values.

▶ **Method 1**

Perimeter of the rectangle = (2 × Length) + (2 × Width)
= (2 × 4) + (2 × 3)
= 8 + 6
= 14 in.

The perimeter of the rectangle is 14 inches.

▶ Method 2

Perimeter of the rectangle = 2 × (Length + Width)
= 2 × (4 + 3)
= 2 × 7
= 14 in.

The perimeter of the rectangle is 14 inches.

2 The length of a side of a square is 6 centimeters.
Find the perimeter of the square.

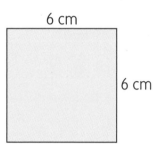

6 cm

6 cm

A square has 4 equal sides.
So, the perimeter of the square
is 4 times the length of its side.

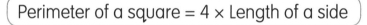

Perimeter of a square = 4 × Length of a side

Perimeter of the square = 4 × 6
= 24 cm

The perimeter of the square is 24 centimeters.

Find the perimeter of the rectangle.

7 ft

4 ft

▶ **Method 1**

Perimeter of the rectangle = (2 × _____) + (2 × _____)

= _____ + _____

= _____ ft

▶ **Method 2**

Perimeter of the rectangle = 2 × (_____ + _____)

= 2 × _____

= _____ ft

Find the perimeter of the square.

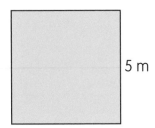

5 m

Perimeter of the square = 4 × _____

= _____ m

Solve. Show your work.

3 A rectangular pool has a length of 15 meters and a width of 8 meters. What is the perimeter of the pool?

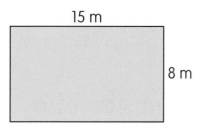

15 m

8 m

4 The length of a rectangular field is 32 yards and its width is 9 yards. June ran round the field once. Find the distance June ran.

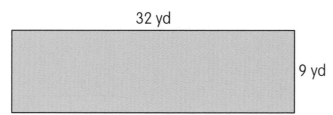

32 yd

9 yd

ENGAGE

Draw a rectangle with a length of 4 centimeters and a perimeter of 12 centimeters on a square grid. What is the width of the rectangle? What are two different ways to find the width? Share your ideas with your partner.

LEARN Find the length of an unknown side of a rectangle or square with known perimeter

1 The perimeter of a rectangle is 18 feet. Its length is 6 feet. Find the width of the rectangle.

▶ **Method 1**

$$\text{Length} + \text{Width} = \text{Perimeter} \div 2$$
$$= 18 \div 2$$
$$= 9 \text{ ft}$$

$$\text{Length} + \text{Width} = 9$$
$$6 + \text{Width} = 9$$
$$\text{Width} = 9 - 6$$
$$= 3 \text{ ft}$$

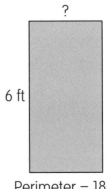

6 ft

?

Perimeter = 18 ft

The width of the rectangle is 3 feet.

▶ **Method 2**

$$\text{Width} + \text{Width} = 18 - 6 - 6$$
$$= 6 \text{ ft}$$

$$\text{Width} = 6 \div 2$$
$$= 3 \text{ ft}$$

The width of the rectangle is 3 feet.

6 + width + 6 + width = 18

2 The perimeter of a square is 64 meters. Find the length of a side of the square.

?

Perimeter = 64 m

A square has 4 equal sides.

Length of a side = Perimeter ÷ 4
$$= 64 ÷ 4$$
$$= 16 \text{ m}$$

The length of a side of the square is 16 meters.

Math Talk

The square and the rectangle have the same perimeter. Discuss with your partner how to find the length of the rectangle in different ways.

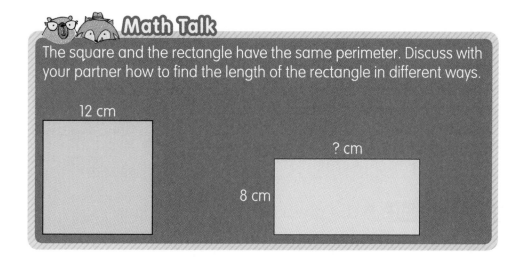

12 cm

? cm

8 cm

Work in pairs.

(1) Draw a rectangle with a length of 8 centimeters and a perimeter of 30 centimeters on a 1-centimeter square grid.

(2) Ask your partner to find the width of the rectangle.

(3) Record the width in the table below.

(4) Take turns repeating (1) to (3) for each rectangle in the table.

Rectangle	Length	Width	Perimeter
A	8 cm		30 cm
B	9 cm		30 cm
C	10 cm		30 cm
D	11 cm		30 cm
E	8 cm		24 cm
F	4 cm		16 cm
G	7 cm		28 cm

(5) **Mathematical Habit 6** Use precise mathematical language
What do you notice about Rectangle F and Rectangle G?

TRY Practice finding the length of an unknown side of a rectangle or square with known perimeter

Solve.

1. The perimeter of a rectangle is 28 yards. The width of the rectangle is 6 yards. Find the length of the rectangle.

▶ **Method 1**

Length + Width = Perimeter ÷ 2

= _____ ÷ _____

= _____ yd

Length + 6 = _____

Length = _____ – _____

= _____ yd

The length of the rectangle is _____ yards.

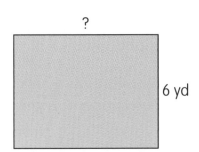

?

6 yd

Perimeter = 28 yd

▶ **Method 2**

Length + Length

= _____ – _____ – _____

= _____ yd

Length

= _____ ÷ _____

= _____ yd

The length of the rectangle is _____ yards.

Length + 6 + Length + 6 = 28

2 Ana bent a wire of 132 centimeters long into a square. What is the length of a side of the square?

?

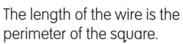

The length of the wire is the perimeter of the square.

Length of a side = _____ ÷ _____

= _____ cm

The length of a side of the square is _____ centimeters.

3 The perimeter of a rectangular pool is 32 yards. The length of the pool is 11 yards. Find the width of the pool.

11 yd

?

4 The perimeter of a square gymnasium is 36 yards. Find the length of one side of the gymnasium.

?

ENGAGE

Draw four different rectangles on a square grid. Use a table to make a list of length and width of each rectangle. Find the area of each rectangle. Discuss the relationship between the length and the area with your partner. What pattern do you notice?

LEARN Find the area of a rectangle or square using a formula

1 The length of a rectangle is 5 centimeters. The width of the rectangle is 3 centimeters. Find the area of the rectangle.

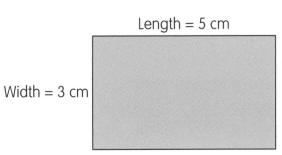

Length = 5 cm

Width = 3 cm

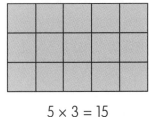

You can multiply the side lengths of a rectangle to find the area.

$5 \times 3 = 15$

Area of a rectangle = Length × Width

Area of the rectangle = 5 × 3
                     = 15 cm²

The area of the rectangle is 15 square centimeters.

2 The length of a side of a square is 3 meters. Find the area of the square.

3 m

Each side of a
square is equal.

Area of a square = Length of a side × Length of a side

Area of the square = 3 × 3
= 9 m²

The area of the square is 9 square meters.

Hands-on Activity Finding areas of squares of different sizes

Work in pairs.

1 Draw and cut out a square with a side length of 1 centimeter.

2 Ask your partner to find the area of the square in **1**.

3 Take turns repeating **1** and **2** using each of the other side lengths.
Complete each table.

Side Length	Area
1 cm	
2 cm	
3 cm	
4 cm	
5 cm	

Side Length	Area
6 cm	
7 cm	
8 cm	
9 cm	
10 cm	

TRY Practice finding the area of a rectangle or square using a formula

Solve.

1 The length of the rectangle is 8 feet. The width of the rectangle is 2 feet. What is the area of the rectangle?

8 ft

2 ft

Area of the rectangle = Length × Width

= _____ × _____

= _____ ft^2

The area of the rectangle is _____ square feet.

2 The length of a side of a square is 7 inches. Find the area of the square.

7 in.

Area of the square = Length of side × Length of side

= _____ × _____

= _____ in^2

The area of the square is _____ square inches.

Find the area of each rectangle.

3

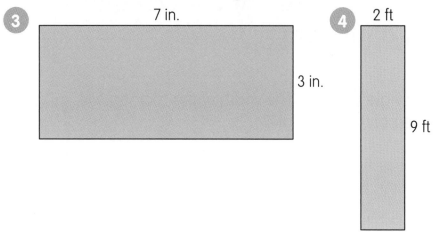

7 in.

3 in.

4

2 ft

9 ft

Find the area of each square.

5

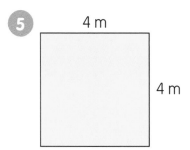

4 m

4 m

6

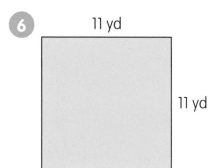

11 yd

11 yd

Solve.

7 Melanie bent a 36-inch wire to make a square photo frame.
What is the area inside the photo frame?

The length of the wire is the perimeter of the frame.

Length of a side = _____ ÷ _____

= _____ in.

Area inside the photo frame = _____ × _____

= _____ in²

The area inside the photo frame is _____ square inches.

8 The perimeter of a square garden is 24 meters.
Find the area of the garden.

ENGAGE

If all the sides are whole numbers, find the missing lengths of the figure. What is the greatest possible length of *AB*?

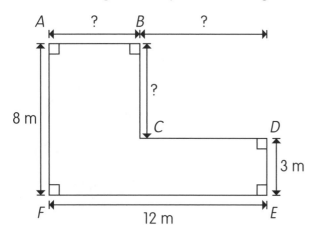

LEARN Find the length of an unknown side of a rectangle or square with known area

1 The area of a rectangular carpet is 63 square meters. The length of the carpet is 9 meters. Find the width of the carpet.

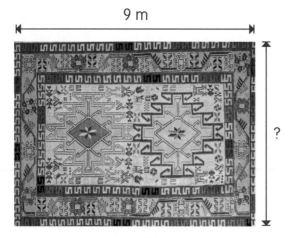

Area = 63 m²

Length × Width = Area of the carpet

$$9 \times \text{Width} = 63$$
$$\text{Width} = 63 \div 9$$
$$= 7 \text{ m}$$

The width of the carpet is 7 meters.

2 The area of a square is 25 square inches.
  a Find the length of a side of the square.
  b Find the perimeter of the square.

$$\boxed{\begin{array}{c} ? \\ \text{Area} = 25 \text{ in}^2 \end{array}}$$

  a Area = Length of a side × Length of a side
     25 = 5 × 5
     Length of a side = 5 in.

  The length of a side of the square is 5 inches.

  b Perimeter of the square = 4 × Length of a side
                    = 4 × 5
                    = 20 in.

  The perimeter of the square is 20 inches.

Hands-on Activity Finding the unknown side of a rectangle with known area

Work in pairs.

1 Draw a rectangle with a length of 4 centimeters and an area of 12 square centimeters on a 1-centimeter square grid.

2 Find the width of the rectangle and record it in the table.

3 Repeat 1 and 2 using each of the other lengths and areas in the table. Complete the table.

Rectangle	Length	Width	Area
A	4 cm		12 cm²
B	8 cm		48 cm²
C	6 cm		30 cm²

TRY Practice finding the unknown side of a rectangle or square with known area

Find the unknown side of each rectangle or square.

1. The area of a rectangular garden is 72 square feet. The width of the garden is 8 feet. What is the length of the garden?

   Length × 8 = _____

      Length = _____ ÷ _____

          = _____ ft

   The length of the garden is 9 feet.

?

8 ft   Area = 72 ft^2

2. The area of a square is 64 square inches.
   a Find the length of a side of the square.
   b Find the perimeter of the square.

   a   _____ = _____ × _____

     Length of a side = _____ in.

     The length of a side of the square is _____ inches.

   b Perimeter of the square = 4 × _____

                   = _____ in.

     The perimeter of the square is _____ inches.

?

Area = 64 in^2

INDEPENDENT PRACTICE

Find the perimeter and area of each rectangle.

1
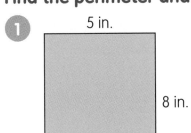
5 in.

8 in.

2
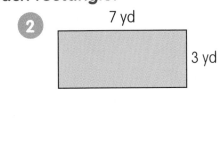
7 yd

3 yd

Find the perimeter and area of each square.

3
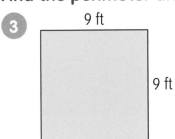
9 ft

9 ft

4
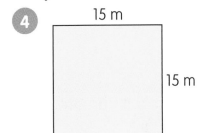
15 m

15 m

Solve.

5 The perimeter of a rectangular room is 24 meters. The width of the room is 4 meters. Find the length of the room.

6 The area of a rectangular playground is 84 square yards. The width of the playground is 7 yards. What is the length of the playground?

7 Gael drew a square with an area of 36 square centimeters. Find the length of a side of the square.

8   The perimeter of a piece of paper is 38 inches. Its length is 11 inches.
    a   Find the width of the piece of paper.

    b   Find the area of the piece of paper.

9   The perimeter of a square room is 48 yards.
    a   Find the length of a side of the room.

    b   Find the area of the room.

10 The area of a rectangular pool is 225 square meters. The width of the pool is 9 meters.

  a Find the length of the pool.

  b Find the perimeter of the pool.

11 The area of a square tray is 81 square inches.

  a Find the length of a side of the tray.

  b Find the perimeter of the tray.

2 Composite Figures

Learning Objectives:
- Find the perimeter of a composite figure.
- Find the area of a composite figure.

New Vocabulary
composite figure

THINK

The area of a square is 81 square centimeters. A rectangle is cut from the square. The area of the remaining part is 25 square centimeters. If the sides of the rectangle are whole numbers, find the perimeter of the rectangle that was cut out.

ENGAGE

The length of Rectangle A is 4 cm longer than the length of Rectangle B but their perimeters are the same. How is this possible? Explore all possibilities using a geoboard. Explain how you arrive at your answer.

Use a geoboard to explore all possibilities.

LEARN Find the perimeter of a composite figure

1 Ms. Jones wants to put up a fence around a piece of land as shown. What is the perimeter of the piece of land?

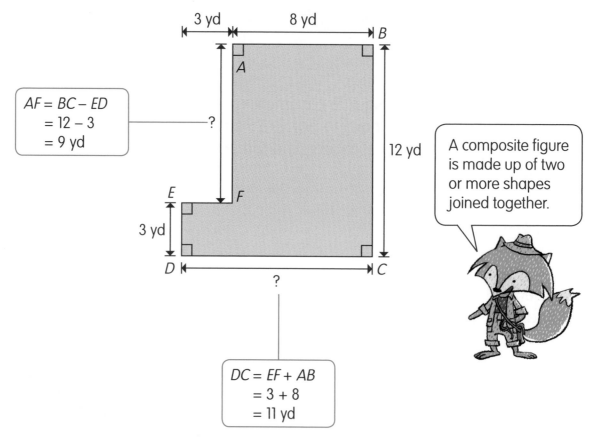

$AF = BC - ED$
$= 12 - 3$
$= 9$ yd

A composite figure is made up of two or more shapes joined together.

$DC = EF + AB$
$= 3 + 8$
$= 11$ yd

Perimeter of the piece of land $= AB + BC + CD + DE + EF + FA$
$= 8 + 12 + 11 + 3 + 3 + 9$
$= 46$ yd

The perimeter of the piece of land is 46 yards.

Math Talk

What do you notice about the total lengths of *DE* and *FA*, and *EF* and *AB*? What is another way to find the perimeter of the figure?

TRY Practice finding the perimeter of a composite figure

Fill in each blank.

1 Find the perimeter of Figure *ABCDEFGH*.

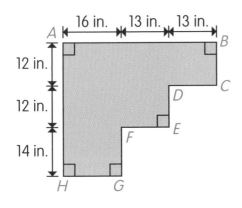

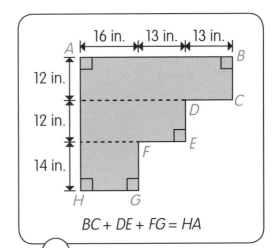

BC + DE + FG = HA

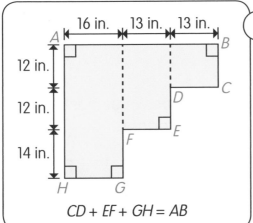

CD + EF + GH = AB

$AB = \_\_\_\_ + \_\_\_\_ + \_\_\_\_$

$ = \_\_\_\_$ in.

$HA = \_\_\_\_ + \_\_\_\_ + \_\_\_\_$

$ = \_\_\_\_$ in.

Perimeter of Figure *ABCDEFGH*

$= AB + \_\_\_\_ + \_\_\_\_ + \_\_\_\_ + \_\_\_\_ + \_\_\_\_ + \_\_\_\_ + \_\_\_\_$

$= \_\_\_\_ + \_\_\_\_ + \_\_\_\_ + \_\_\_\_ + \_\_\_\_ + \_\_\_\_ + \_\_\_\_ + \_\_\_\_$

$= \_\_\_\_$ in.

The perimeter of Figure *ABCDEFGH* is _____ inches.

Find the perimeter of the figure.

2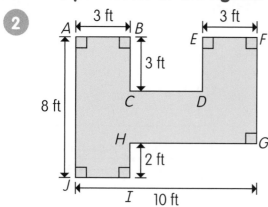

ENGAGE

Divide each figure below into rectangles and/or squares in at least two different ways. Share your divided figures with your partner.

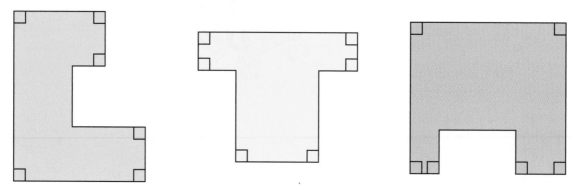

LEARN Find the area of a composite figure

1. Rectangle C is cut out from a rectangular cardboard measuring 10 inches by 8 inches. Find the area of the remaining cardboard.

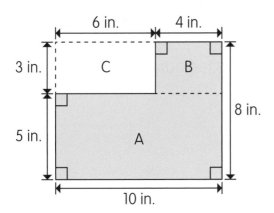

▶ **Method 1**

Area of remaining cardboard = Area of A + Area of B
Area of A = 10 × 5
       = 50 in²
Area of B = 4 × 3
       = 12 in²
Area of the remaining cardboard = 50 + 12
                = 62 in²

The area of the remaining cardboard is 62 square inches.

▶ **Method 2**

Area of remaining cardboard = Area of cardboard – Area of C
Area of cardboard = 10 × 8
          = 80 in²
Area of C = 6 × 3
       = 18 in²
Area of the remaining cardboard = 80 – 18
                = 62 in²

The area of the remaining cardboard is 62 square inches.

Hands-on Activity

Work in pairs.

Activity 1 Forming a composite figure and finding its area and perimeter

1. Use cut-outs provided by your teacher to form a composite figure. Paste the figure below.

2. Find the area and perimeter of the composite figure.

Activity 2 Finding the area and perimeter of a composite figure by dividing it into rectangles and squares

(1) Draw a composite figure on the square grid paper below.

(2) Find the perimeter of the figure.

(3) Use Method 1 on page 133 to find the area of the figure.

(4) Exchange composite figures with your partner. Ask your partner to use Method 2 on page 133 to find the area of the figure.

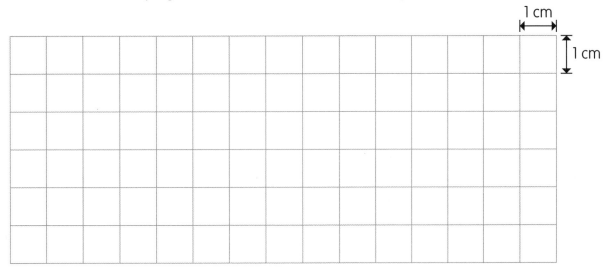

1 cm

1 cm

Perimeter =

▶ **Method 1**

▶ **Method 2**

TRY Practice finding the area of a composite figure

Fill in each blank.

1 A smaller square is cut out from a larger square. Find the area of the shaded part.

▶ **Method 1**

Area of the shaded part = Area of _____ + Area of _____

Area of _____ = _____ ◯ _____

= _____ in²

Area of _____ = _____ ◯ _____

= _____ in²

Area of the shaded part = _____ ◯ _____

= _____ in²

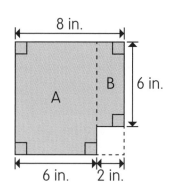

▶ **Method 2**

Area of the shaded part = Area of larger square − Area of smaller square

Area of the larger square = _____ ◯ _____

= _____ in²

Area of the smaller square = _____ ◯ _____

= _____ in²

Area of the shaded part = _____ ◯ _____

= _____ in²

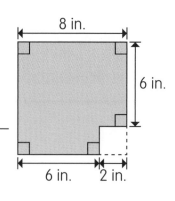

Find the area of each figure.

2

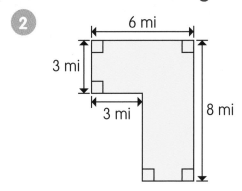

3

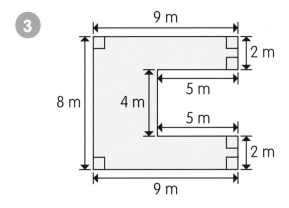

4

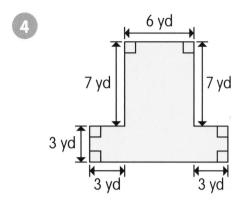

5

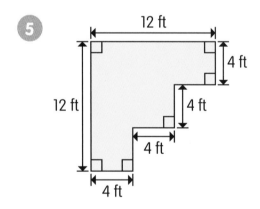

INDEPENDENT PRACTICE

Find the perimeter and area of each composite figure.

1

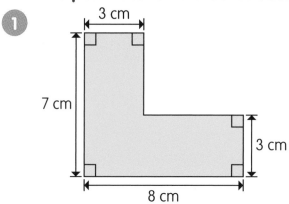

2

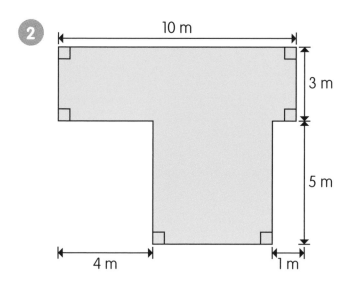

3

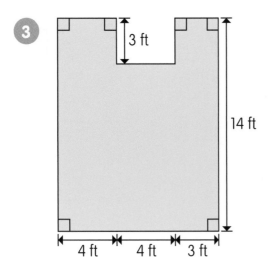

3 ft

14 ft

4 ft   4 ft   3 ft

4

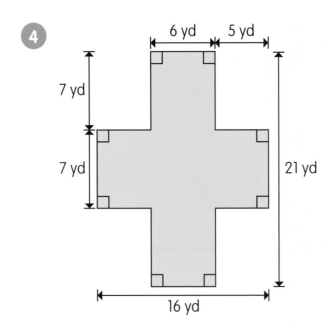

6 yd   5 yd

7 yd

7 yd

21 yd

16 yd

3 Real-World Problems: Area and Perimeter

Learning Objective:
- Solve real-world problems involving area and perimeter of composite figures.

THINK

A large rectangle is divided into 4 smaller rectangles as shown. The area of Rectangle A is 15 square inches and the area of Rectangle B is 28 square inches. Find the perimeter and area of the large rectangle.

ENGAGE

Sara's garden measures 12 yards by 9 yards. The garden has a rectangular flower bed in the middle of it. The flower bed is surrounded by a stone path 1 yard wide.

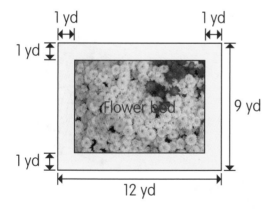

Find the length and width of the flower bed and use them to find the area of the flower bed.

LEARN Solve real-world problems involving area and perimeter of composite figures

1 A rectangular piece of fabric measures 30 inches by 20 inches. When the fabric is placed on a rectangular table, it leaves a margin of 2 inches wide all around it. Find the area of the table that is not covered by the fabric.

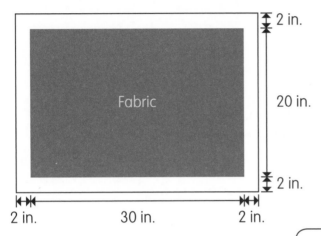

2 in.

20 in.

2 in.

2 in.   30 in.   2 in.

Area of the table that is not covered by fabric = Area of the table – Area of the fabric

STEP 1 Understand the problem.

What is the area of the piece of fabric? What is the length and width of the table? What is the area of the table? What do I need to find?

STEP 2 Think of a plan.
I can use a formula.

STEP 3 ▶ Carry out the plan.
Length of the table = 2 + 30 + 2
= 34 in.

Width of the table = 2 + 20 + 2
= 24 in.

Area of the table = 34 × 24
= 816 in^2

Area of the fabric = 30 × 20
= 600 in^2

Area of the table that is not covered by the fabric = 816 − 600
= 216 in^2

The area of the table that is not covered by the fabric is 216 square inches.

STEP 4 ▶ Check the answer.
I can work backwards to check my answer.

> Area of the table that is not covered by the fabric = 216 in^2
> Area of the fabric = 600 in^2
> Area of the table = 600 + 216
> = 816 in^2
> So, my answer is correct.

TRY Practice solving real-world problems involving area and perimeter of composite figures

Fill in each blank.

1 The figure shows a rectangular field with a path 2 meters wide around it. Find the area of the path.

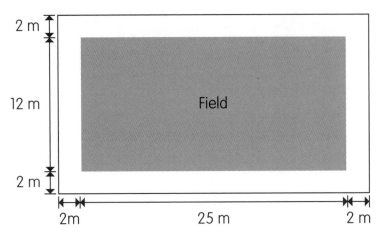

Length of the large rectangle = _____ ◯ _____ ◯ _____

= _____ m

Width of the large rectangle = _____ ◯ _____ ◯ _____

= _____ m

Area of the rectangle = _____ ◯ _____

= _____ m²

Area of the small rectangle = _____ ◯ _____

= _____ m²

Area of the path = _____ ◯ _____

= _____ m²

Area of the path
= Area of the large rectangle
  − Area of the small rectangle

The area of the path is _____ square meters.

2 The figure shows a small rectangle cut out from a larger rectangle *ADEF*. Find the area of the shaded part of the figure.

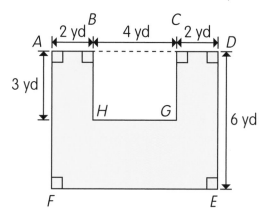

Length of the large rectangle = _____ ⬭ _____ ⬭ _____

= _____ yd

Width of the large rectangle = _____ yd

Area of the large rectangle = _____ ⬭ _____

= _____ yd²

Area of the small rectangle = _____ ⬭ _____

= _____ yd²

Area of the shaded part = _____ ⬭ _____

= _____ yd²

The area of the shaded part of the figure is _____ square yards.

3 There is a 2-yard wide path around a rectangular piece of land.
   The length and width of the path are shown in the figure.

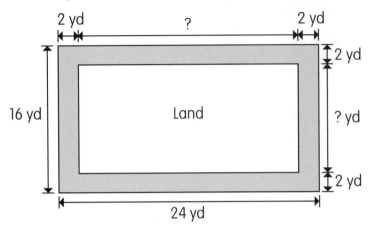

a Find the area of the land.

b Find the perimeter of the land.

Each figure has been made by folding its original figure.

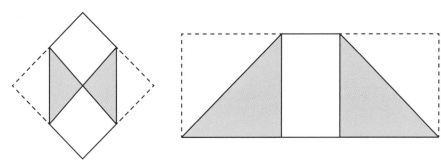

Draw each original figure.

LEARN Find the area and perimeter of parts of a figure

1 A corner of a square piece of paper is folded.

a Find the area of the shaded part.
The shaded part is half of a 2-inch square.

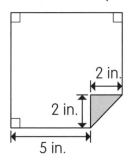

Area of 2-inch square = 2 × 2
= 4 in²

Area of the shaded part = 4 ÷ 2
= 2 in²

The area of the shaded part is 2 square inches.

b Find the perimeter of the square piece of paper unfolded.

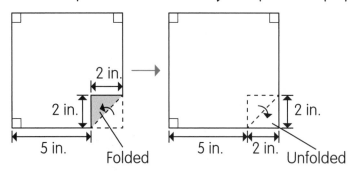

Folded   Unfolded

To find the perimeter of the square piece of paper unfolded, you need to find the length of a side of the square.

Length of a side = 5 + 2
= 7 in.

Perimeter of the square = 4 × 7
= 28 in.

The perimeter of the square piece of paper is 28 inches.

Math Talk

A square is folded into halves twice.

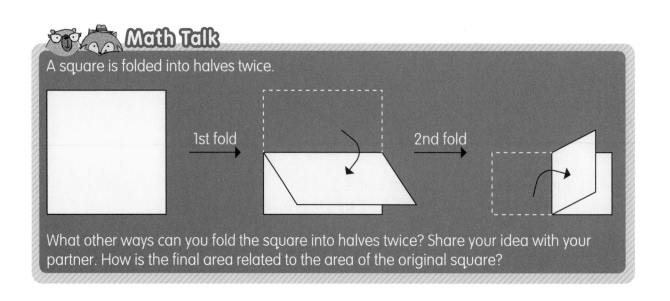

1st fold   2nd fold

What other ways can you fold the square into halves twice? Share your idea with your partner. How is the final area related to the area of the original square?

TRY Practice finding the area and perimeter of parts of a figure

Solve.

1 A rectangular piece of paper is folded at one of its corners so that the side *BC* lies along the side *CD* as shown.

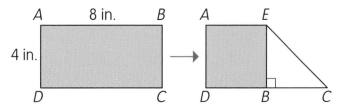

a Find the area of the rectangular piece of paper before it was folded.

b Find the area of the figure after the paper was folded.

1. Draw a rectangle with a length of 8 centimeters and a width of 6 centimeters on centimeter grid paper.

2. Label the length and width. Find the area.

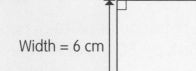

3. Cut out the rectangle.

4. Fold the cut-out rectangle to make a rectangle of a different size. Measure the length and width of this shape. Then, find the area.

Example

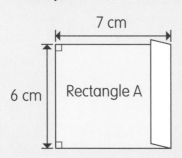

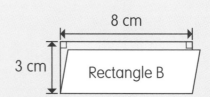

5. Unfold the rectangle you made in ④. Fold it to make another rectangular shape. This time take only one measurement — measure the side that is changed by the folding. Then, find the area of the folded rectangle.

6. Check your answer by measuring the length and width of the folded rectangle.

7. Make two more rectangles with the cutout. Take only one measurement for each rectangle as in ⑤. Then, find its area. Does your method of using one measurement to find the area apply to these rectangles too?

INDEPENDENT PRACTICE

Solve.

1 The figure below shows a cattle yard on a farm. Find the length of the cattle fence around the perimeter of the yard.

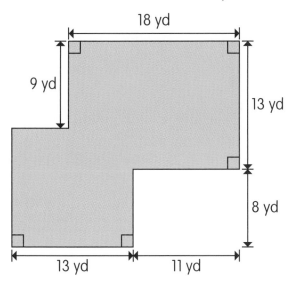

2 Brandon is laying a carpet on the floor of a rectangular room. The border around the carpet is 1 meter wide. Find the area of the floor that is not covered by the carpet.

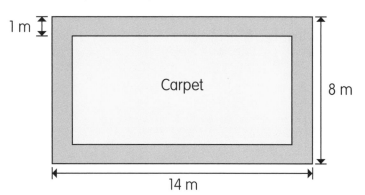

3 Carter has a rectangular sheet of paper with a length of 13 inches and a width of 8 inches. He cuts away a small rectangle at one of its corners. The length and width of the small rectangle are shown in the figure.

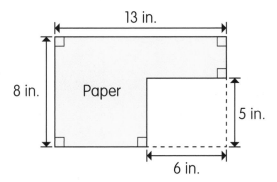

a Find the remaining area of the paper.

b Find the perimeter of the remaining paper.

4 Mia had a rectangular piece of paper. She folded two of the corners as shown.

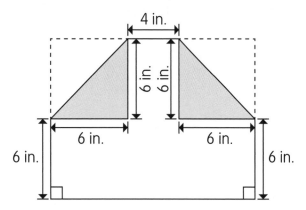

a Find the perimeter of the rectangular piece of paper before the corners were folded.

b Find the area of the figure after the corners were folded.

Mathematical Habit 6 Use precise mathematical language

The area of a square is given. Kimberly says that to find the length of one side, she can divide the area by 4. Is Kimberly correct? If not, explain to Kimberly how to find the length of one side of the square.

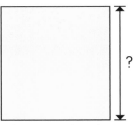

(Area is given)

Mathematical Habit 6 Use precise mathematical language

1 What is the length of one side of a square if its perimeter and area have the same numerical value?

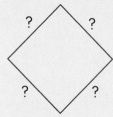

Side length (yd)	Perimeter (yd)	Area (yd²)	Perimeter = Area?

2 The side of a small square is 5 inches. Hana uses 36 of these squares to form a large square. What is the area of the large square?

3 Mr. Clark had a large square tile with a side length of 12 centimeters. He painted 3 identical smaller squares across the tile as shown. Find the area of the unpainted parts of the square.

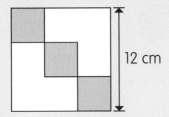

12 cm

CHAPTER WRAP-UP ?

How do you find the perimeter and area of a rectangle or square using a formula? How do you find an unknown side of a rectangle or square, given its area or perimeter?

Area and Perimeter

Use Formula

Perimeter of a rectangle
= (2 × Length) + (2 × Width)
= 2 × (Length + Width)

Area of a rectangle
= Length × Width

Area of a square
= Length of side × Length of side

Find the unknown side

To find the length of one side of a rectangle given the perimeter and the other side:

▶ **Method 1**

Length + Width = Perimeter ÷ 2

▶ **Method 2**

Length + Length
= Perimeter – Width – Width

To find the length of a side of a square given the perimeter:
Length of a side = Perimeter ÷ 4

To find the length of one side of a rectangle given the area and the other side:
Length = Area ÷ Width

To find the length of a side of a square given the area:
Length of side × Length of side = Area

Composite Figure

To find the perimeter of a composite figure, first find the unknown lengths. Then, find its perimeter.

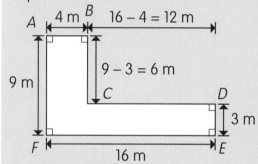

Perimeter = 9 + 4 + 6 + 12 + 3 + 16
= 50 m

To find the area of a composite figure, first divide the composite figure into rectangle(s) and/or square(s). Then, find its area.

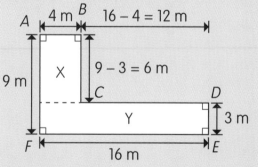

Area of X = 6 × 4
= 24 m²
Area of Y = 16 × 3
= 48 m²
Area of the figure = 24 + 48
= 72 m²

Find the perimeter and area of the rectangle.

1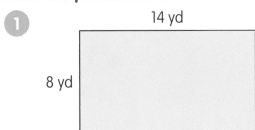

Find the perimeter and area of the square.

2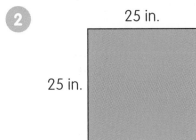

Find the length and area of the rectangle.

3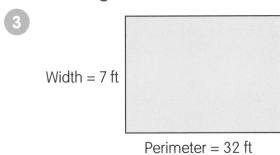

Find the length of a side of the square. Then, find the perimeter of the square.

4

Area = 81 cm²

Find the area and perimeter of each composite figure.

5

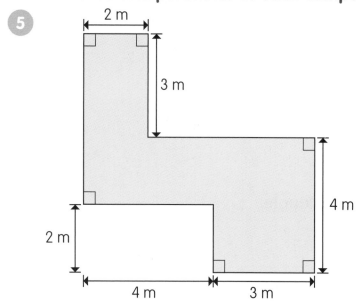

2 m

3 m

2 m

4 m

4 m

3 m

6

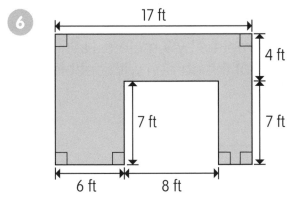

Solve.

7 Bruno's rectangular garden measures 12 meters by 9 meters. He filled up a 1-meter pathway around the border of the garden with pebbles. What is the area covered by the pebbles?

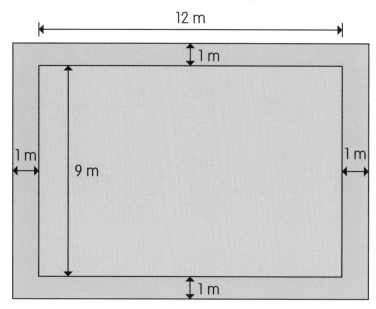

Assessment Prep

Answer each question.

8 The area of a rectangular field is 117 square yards.
The width of the field is 9 yards. What is the length of the field?

Width = 9 yd

(A) 9 yards

(B) 13 yards

(C) 22 yards

(D) 44 yards

9 A square piece of paper has a perimeter of 60 centimeters. María cuts
away a 5-centimeter wide rectangular strip along one side of the paper
as shown. What is the area of the remaining piece of paper?

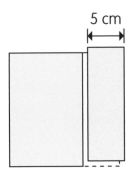

5 cm

(A) 75 square centimeters

(B) 150 square centimeters

(C) 225 square centimeters

(D) 300 square centimeters

10 A rectangular piece of cardboard measures 24 inches by 14 inches. Matthew places a photograph on the cardboard such that there is a 2-inch border around the photograph. What is the area covered by the photograph?

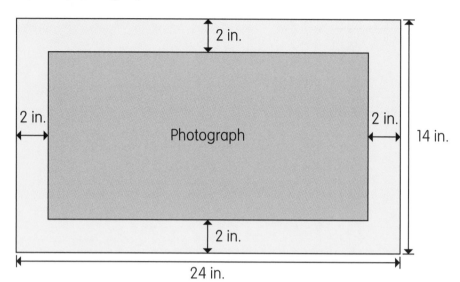

A Community Garden

1 Ms. Adams uses some rectangular cards to make labels for the plants in her garden. Each rectangular card has an area of 32 square centimeters. The length of the card is twice its width. What is the length and width of each rectangular card? Show your work.

Area = 32 cm^2

2 **a** Draw two different rectangles that have an area of 16 square units each. Label your drawings to show the length and width of each rectangle.

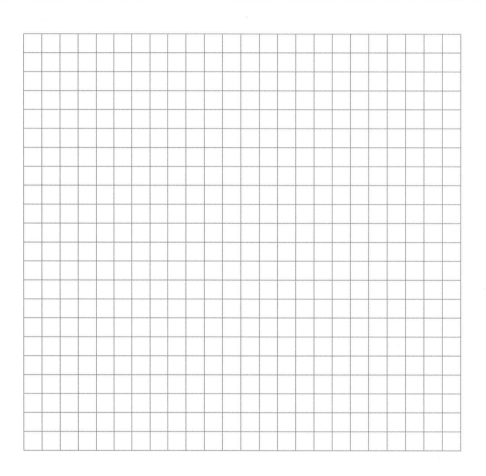

b Find the perimeter of each rectangle that you drew. Compare how the perimeters relate to the shapes of the two rectangles.

3 The figure below shows Mr. Garcia's garden.

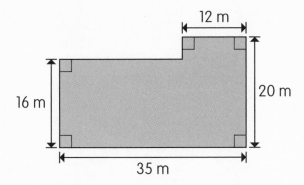

a What is the perimeter of the garden?
Show your work.

b What is the area of the garden?
Show your work.

4 Mr. Roberts is setting up a community garden.
The community garden contains 9 similar plots, as shown.
Each plot has the same size as Mr. Parker's plot.

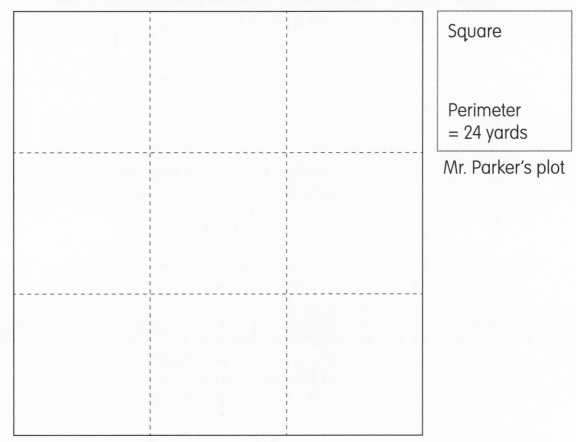

Square

Perimeter
= 24 yards

Mr. Parker's plot

Community Garden

Mr. Roberts needs enough fencing for the perimeter of the garden.
How much fencing, in yards, does he need to buy?
Show your work.

Rubric

Point(s)	Level	My Performance
7–8	4	• Most of my answers are correct. • I showed complete understanding of what I have learned. • I used the correct strategies to solve the problems. • I explained my answers and mathematical thinking clearly and completely.
5–6	3	• Some of my answers are correct. • I showed some understanding of what I have learned. • I used some correct strategies to solve the problems. • I explained my answers and mathematical thinking clearly.
3–4	2	• A few of my answers are correct. • I showed little understanding of what I have learned. • I used a few correct strategies to solve the problems. • I explained some of my answers and mathematical thinking clearly.
0–2	1	• A few of my answers are correct. • I showed little or no understanding of what I have learned. • I used a few strategies to solve the problems. • I did not explain my answers and mathematical thinking clearly.

Teacher's Comments

Chapter 7

Angles and Line Segments

T-SHIRT DESIGN COMPETITION

The winning design has angles that are less than a right angle, and greater than a right angle. What are these angles called?

How can you measure and draw angles? How can you draw perpendicular and parallel line segments?

Name: _____ Date: _____

Defining a point, a line, and a line segment

Definition	Example	You Say and Write
A point is an exact location in space.	• B	Point B
A line is a straight path continuing without end in two opposite directions.	←•————•→ C D	Line CD
A line segment is a part of a line with two endpoints.	•————• E F	Line segment EF

▶ **Quick Check**

Complete with point, line, or line segment.

1️⃣ A _____ is an exact location in space.

2️⃣ A _____ is a part of a line with two endpoints.

3️⃣ A _____ is a straight path continuing without end in two opposite directions.

Defining angles

An angle is formed by two line segments with a common endpoint.

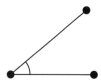

An angle can also be formed when two sides of a figure meet.

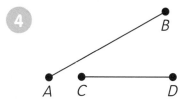

▶ Quick Check

Decide whether each figure forms an angle. Explain your answer.

4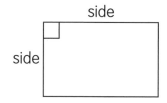

5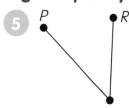

Copy the shapes. Mark an angle in each shape.

6 Rectangle

7 Pentagon

Comparing angles with a right angle

Fold a piece of paper like this to get a right-angled corner.

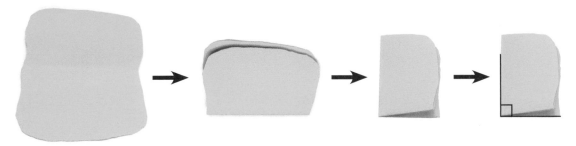

Compare an angle with a right angle.

Use the folded paper to check if the angles are less than or greater than a right angle.

Angle *E* is the same as a right angle.

Angle *F* is less than a right angle.

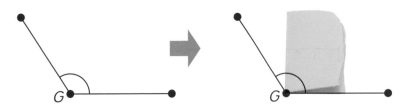

Angle *G* is greater than a right angle.

▶ **Quick Check**

Decide whether the line segments in each angle form a right angle.
Use a piece of folded paper to help you. Explain your answer.

_____   _____   _____

Look at the angles. Then answer the questions.
Use a piece of folded paper to help you.

   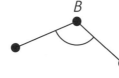

11   Which angles are right angles? _____

12   Which angles measure less than a right angle? _____

13   Which angles measure greater than a right angle? _____

Checking perpendicular lines

Perpendicular lines are two lines that meet at a right angle.

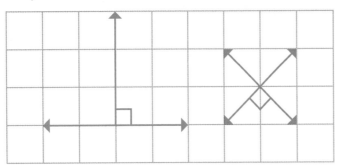

Use a folded sheet of paper or a ruler to check whether two lines are perpendicular.

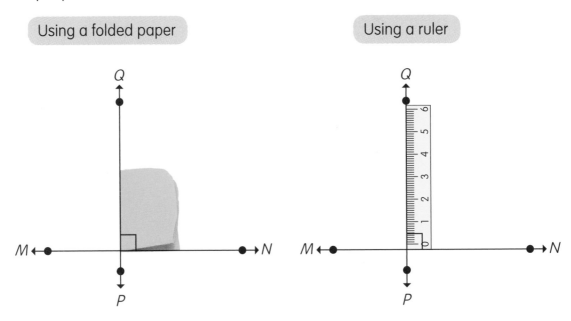

Using a folded paper

Using a ruler

Line *PQ* is perpendicular to line *MN*.

▶ **Quick Check**

Which pairs of line segments are perpendicular?
Use a folded sheet of paper or straightedge to check.

⑭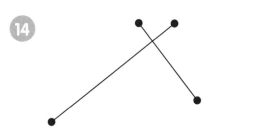

⑮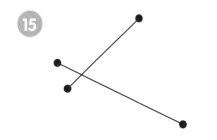

⑯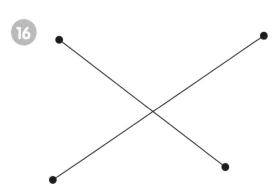

⑰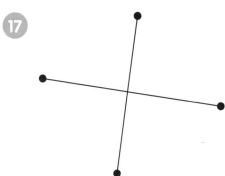

Checking parallel lines

Parallel lines are a set of lines that will never meet no matter how long they are drawn. They are always the same distance apart.

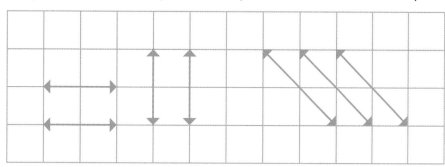

▶ **Quick Check**

Which pairs of line segments are parallel?

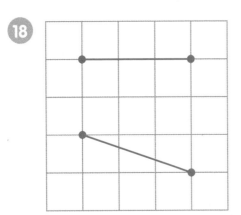

18

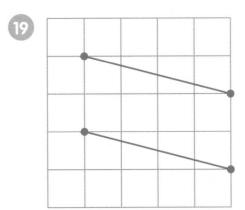

19

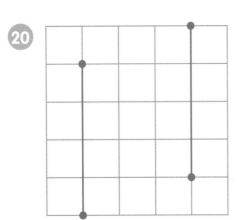

20

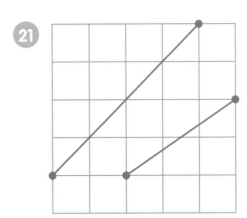

21

Finding perpendicular and/or parallel lines

These are perpendicular line segments in everyday objects.

These are parallel lines in everyday objects.

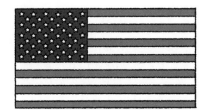

▶ **Quick Check**

Complete with perpendicular **or** parallel.

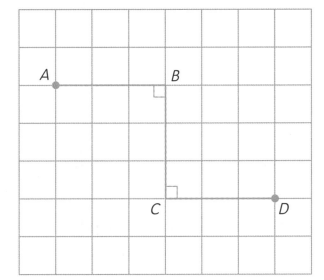

22 Line segment *AB* is _____ to Line segment *CD*.

23 Line segment *AB* is _____ to Line segment *BC*.

24 Line segment *BC* is _____ to Line segment *CD*.

Name a pair of perpendicular line segments and a pair of parallel line segments.

 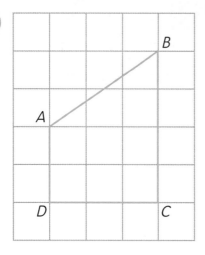

 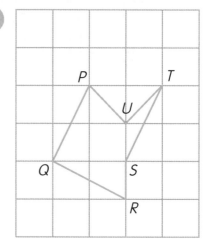

Identify the perpendicular line segments and the parallel line segments on this picture frame.

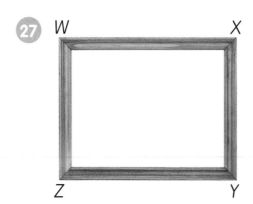

1 Understanding and Measuring Angles

Learning Objectives:
- Identify and name angles.
- Estimate and measure angles.

> **New Vocabulary**
> ray   degrees
> protractor   outer scale
> inner scale   acute angle
> obtuse angle

THINK

Avery draws a quadrilateral *ABCD*.
Two opposite angles are less than 90° each and the other two angles are greater than 90° each. Sketch at least two possible quadrilaterals that Avery drew.

ENGAGE

Look at these shapes.

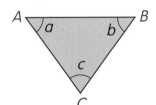
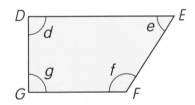

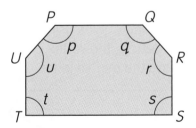

How many angles are there inside each shape?
Name three angles of each shape using small letters.
Suggest other ways to name each angle.
Explain how you do it.

LEARN Use letters to name rays and angles

1 A ray is part of a line that continues without end in one direction. It has one endpoint. You can use two letters to name a ray. The first letter is always the endpoint.

ray *AB*

You can write ray *AB* as $\overrightarrow{AB}$, and ray *BA* as $\overrightarrow{BA}$.

ray *BA*

In the same way, you can write:

a line *CD* or *DC* as $\overleftrightarrow{CD}$ or $\overleftrightarrow{DC}$.

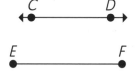

b line segment *EF* or *FE* as $\overline{EF}$ or $\overline{FE}$.

2 $\overrightarrow{PA}$ and $\overrightarrow{PB}$ are rays meeting at point P.

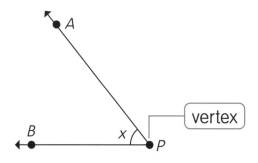

vertex

Name the angle at vertex *P* as ∠*APB* or ∠*BPA*.
If you label the angle at vertex *P* as *x*,
you can also name it ∠*x*.

> In naming angles using three letters, the vertex is always the middle letter.

TRY Practice using letters to name rays and angles

Name the angles.

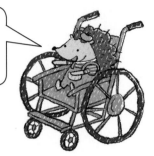

An angle is also formed by two sides of a shape meeting at a point.

1. Angle at *P*: ∠ _____

2. Angle at *Q*: ∠ _____

3. Angle at *R*: ∠ _____

4. Angle at *S*: ∠ _____

Name the angles.

5. 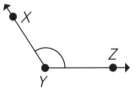   ∠ _____

6. 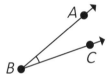   ∠ _____

7. 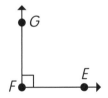   ∠ _____

Name the angles labeled at the vertices *A*, *B*, *C*, and *D* in another way.

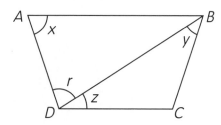

8 ∠x: ∠ _____

9 ∠z: ∠ _____

10 ∠y: ∠ _____

11 ∠r: ∠ _____

ENGAGE

Use two paper strips to form:
a a right angle
b an angle that measures less than a right angle
c an angle that measures more than a right angle

How can you prove the measure of the angles you have created? Share your ideas with your partner.

LEARN Measure angles

1 An angle is measured in **degrees**.
The symbol for degree is °.
A **protractor** is a tool used to measure an angle.

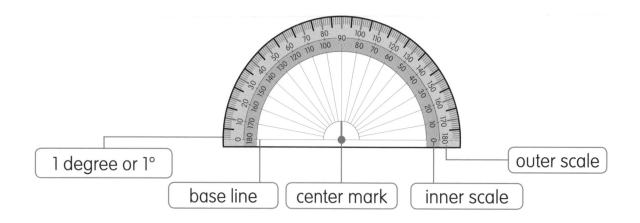

2 Measure ∠BAC.

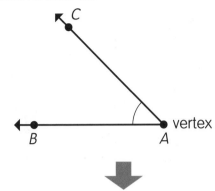

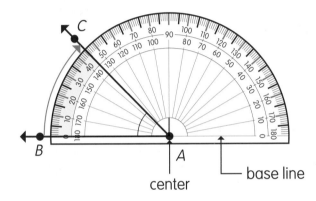

center — base line

STEP **1** Place the base line of the protractor on $\overrightarrow{AB}$.

STEP **2** Place the center of the base line of the protractor at the vertex of the angle.

STEP **3** Read the outer scale. $\overrightarrow{AC}$ passes through the 45° mark.
So, the measure of the angle is 45°.

Since $\overrightarrow{AB}$ passes through the zero mark of the outer scale, read the measure on the outer scale.

3 Measure ∠PQR.

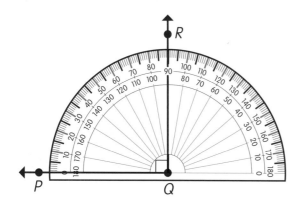

∠PQR is a right angle.

Since $\overrightarrow{QP}$ passes through the zero mark on the outer scale, read the measure on the outer scale.

Measure of ∠PQR = 90°

A right angle has a measure of 90°.

4 Measure ∠DEF.

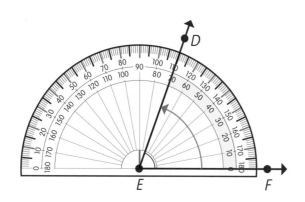

The measure of ∠DEF is less than 90°.

Since $\overrightarrow{EF}$ passes through the zero mark on the inner scale, read the measure on the inner scale.

Measure of ∠DEF = 70°

An angle with a measure less than 90° is an acute angle.

© 2020 Marshall Cavendish Education Pte Ltd

5 Measure ∠JKL.

The measure of ∠JKL is greater than 90°.

Since $\overrightarrow{KJ}$ passes through the zero mark on the outer scale, read the measure on the outer scale.

Measure of ∠JKL = 125°

An angle with a measure greater than 90° but less than 180° is an **obtuse angle**.

Math Talk

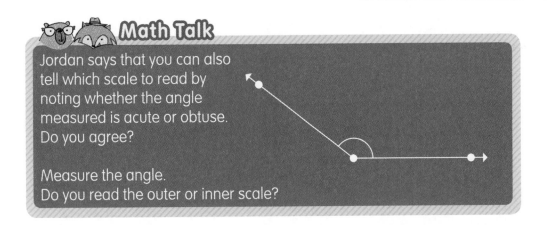

Jordan says that you can also tell which scale to read by noting whether the angle measured is acute or obtuse. Do you agree?

Measure the angle.
Do you read the outer or inner scale?

Work in pairs.

1 Estimate the measure of each angle. Then, use 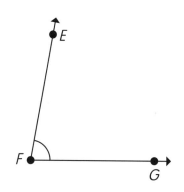 to measure each angle. Decide if each angle is an acute angle, an obtuse angle, or a right angle.

2 Record your answers in the table below. The first one has been done for you.

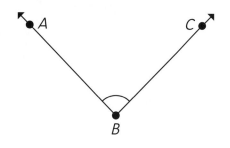

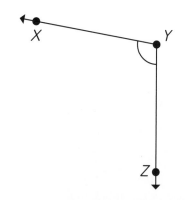

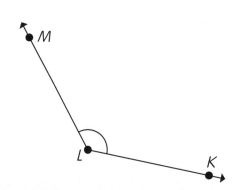

Angle	Estimated Measure	Actual Measure	Type of Angle
∠ABC	80°	90°	Right angle

TRY Practice measuring angles

Fill in each blank.

1 Measure ∠GHK.

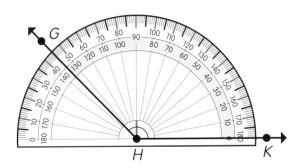

Is ∠GHK an acute angle or an obtuse angle? _____

The measure of ∠GHK is _____ degrees.

Measure of ∠GHK = _____°

Explain when to use the inner scale of the protractor.

2 Measure ∠JKL.

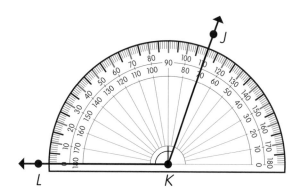

Is ∠JKL an acute angle or an obtuse angle? _____

The measure of ∠JKL is _____ degrees.

Measure of ∠JKL = _____°

Did you read the inner or outer scale? Explain your answer.

Find the measure of each angle.

3

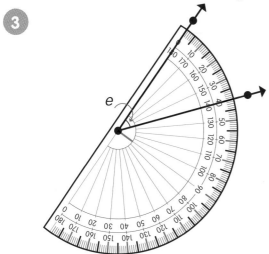

Measure of ∠e = _____°

4

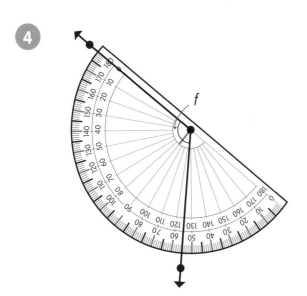

Measure of ∠f = _____°

Use to find the measure of each angle.

5

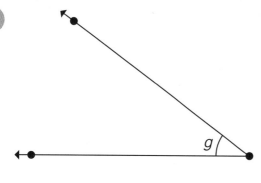

Measure of ∠g = _____°

6

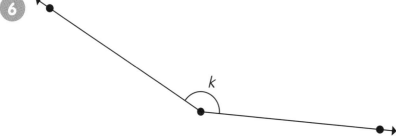

Measure of ∠k = _____°

7

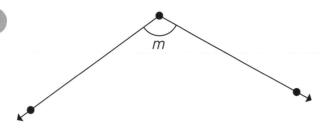

Measure of ∠m = _____°

Name: _____   Date: _____

INDEPENDENT PRACTICE

Look at the angles formed. Fill in each blank.

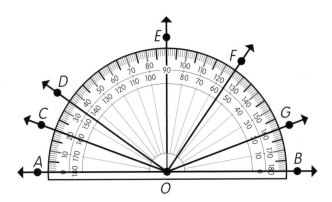

1 Name two angles that are right angles.

∠ _____

∠ _____

2 Name four angles that are acute angles.
What are the measures of these angles?

3 Name four angles that are obtuse angles.
What are the measures of these angles?

Use **to find the measure of each angle.**

4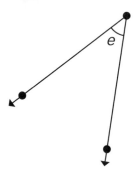

Measure of ∠e = _____°

5

Measure of ∠f = _____°

6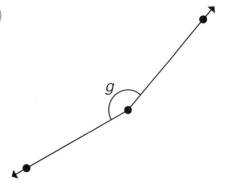

Measure of ∠g = _____°

Use **to measure each marked angle in the shape.**

7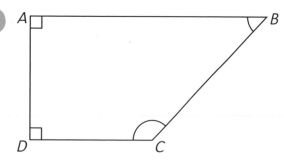

Measure of ∠DAB = _____°   Measure of ∠ABC = _____°

Measure of ∠BCD = _____°   Measure of ∠CDA = _____°

2 Drawing Angles to 180°

Learning Objective:
- Use a protractor to draw angles to 180°.

THINK

Draw a line segment AB 6 centimeters long. At point A, draw an angle of measure of 60°. At point B, draw another angle to form a triangle ABC. What is the least possible length of line segment BC? Explain your thinking to your partner.

ENGAGE

Mark says he can form a line using two acute angles. Joe says he can form a line using one acute and one obtuse angle. Who is correct?
Justify your answer using a grid paper and a protractor.

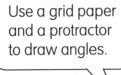

Use a grid paper and a protractor to draw angles.

LEARN Use a protractor to draw angles to 180°

1 You can use 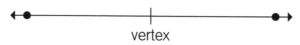 to draw a given angle.

Follow these steps to draw an angle of measure of 70°.

STEP 1 Draw a line and mark a point on the line. This point is the vertex.

vertex

STEP 2 Place the base line of the protractor on the line and the center of the base line on the vertex.

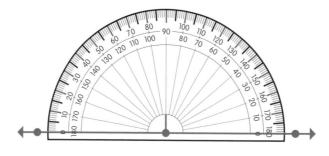

STEP 3 Use the inner scale or the outer scale to find the 70° mark. Mark it with a dot as shown.

Using inner scale   Using outer scale

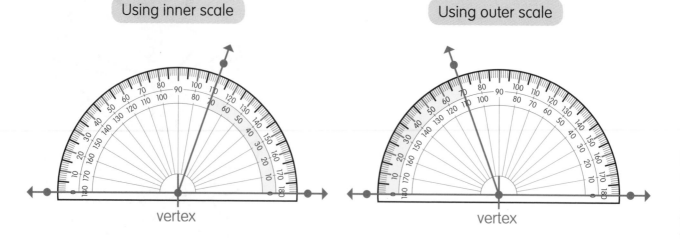

vertex   vertex

Remove the protractor and draw a ray from the vertex through the dot. Then, mark the angle 70°.

2 Draw an angle of 145°.
Remember to start by lining up the vertex and the base line.

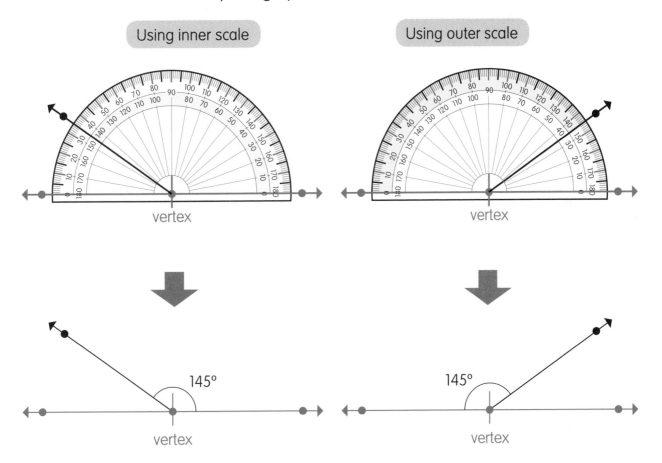

3 Draw a ray and label it $\overrightarrow{AB}$. Using point A as the vertex, draw $\angle CAB$ that measures

a 45° so that $\overrightarrow{AC}$ lies above $\overrightarrow{AB}$.

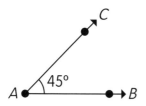

This is an angle above $\overrightarrow{AB}$.

b 45° so that $\overrightarrow{AC}$ lies below $\overrightarrow{AB}$.

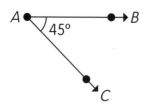

This is an angle below $\overrightarrow{AB}$.

Hands-on Activity Drawing angles

1 Use a ruler and 🔺 to draw each of the following angles on the next page.

| a | 50° | b | 35° | c | 90° | d | 140° |

2 Compare your drawings with your classmates'.
What do you notice?

a   50°

b   35°

c   90°

d   140°

TRY Practice drawing angles to 180°

Use the given to draw each angle.

1. 65° using the inner scale

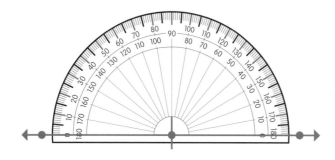

2. 120° using the outer scale

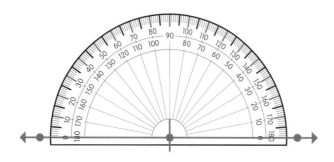

3. 165° using the inner scale

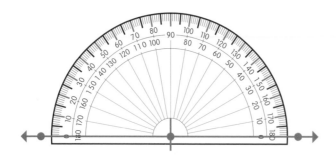

Join the marked endpoint of each ray to one of the dots to form an angle with the given value. Then, label the angle.

4 Measure of ∠b = 80°

    •   •

5 Measure of ∠c = 130°

            •
              •

Use a  to draw each angle.

6 Using point Q as the vertex, draw ∠PQR that measures

    a   55° so that $\overrightarrow{QP}$ lies above $\overrightarrow{QR}$.   b   55° so that $\overrightarrow{QP}$ lies below $\overrightarrow{QR}$.

Q •————————————————•→
                        R

Use $\overrightarrow{MN}$ as one ray of the angle. Draw an angle with the given angle measure.

7 Measure of $\angle LMN = 64°$

Use a ruler and  **to draw an angle with the given angle measure.**

8 158°

INDEPENDENT PRACTICE

Use $\overrightarrow{QP}$ as one ray of each angle. Draw an angle with each given angle measure.

1 Measure of ∠PQR = 81°

P   Q

2 Measure of ∠PQR = 134°

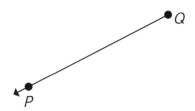

Q

P

Use a ruler and to draw an angle that has each of the following measure.

3 75°

4 163°

3 Turns and Angle Measures

Learning Objectives:
- Relate $\frac{1}{4}$-, $\frac{1}{2}$-, $\frac{3}{4}$-, full turns to the number of right angles (90°).
- Understand what an angle measure of 1° represents.

New Vocabulary
turn
straight angle

THINK

Jason looks at a clock that shows 4 o'clock. After not more than 3 hours, Jason looks at the clock again and the minute hand appears to have turned more than a $\frac{1}{4}$-turn but less than a $\frac{1}{2}$-turn. State at least two possible times that the clock shows now.

ENGAGE

Look at the clock.

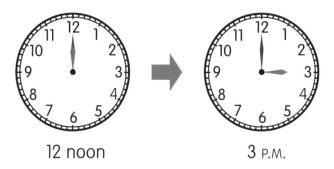

12 noon   3 P.M.

What fraction of the clock did the hour hand turn through from 12 noon to 3 P.M.? What is the measure of the angle that the hour hand turned through?

LEARN Relate turns to right angles and fractional parts of a circle

1 One right angle

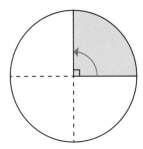

A $\frac{1}{4}$-turn is a measure of 90°.

Two right angles

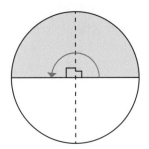

A $\frac{1}{2}$-turn is a measure of 180°.

An angle with a measure of 180° is called a straight angle.

180°

Three right angles

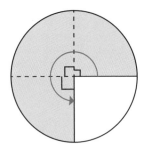

A $\frac{3}{4}$-turn is a measure of 270°.

Four right angles

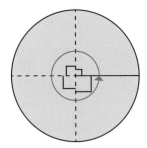

A full turn is a measure of 360°.

Hands-on Activity

Work in pairs.

Activity 1   Relating turns to angle measures

Your teacher will give you two paper strips and a fastener.

1 Paste strip 2 on a piece of drawing paper. Fasten strip 1 onto strip 2 so that only strip 1 moves. This is a pair of angle strips.

2. Turn strip 1 to make each turn below. After each turn, draw the angle formed. Express each turn as a fraction of a full turn and write the measure of each angle. The first one has been done for you.

a A $\frac{1}{4}$-turn

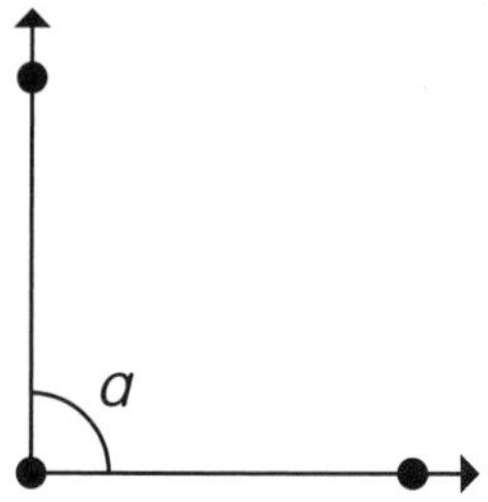

$\frac{1}{4}$-turn

one right angle

$\frac{1}{4} = \frac{90}{360}$

Measure of $\angle a = 90°$

b A $\frac{1}{2}$-turn

c A $\frac{3}{4}$-turn

d A full turn

③ Draw an acute angle, an obtuse angle and a straight angle with your partner. Explain how each angle is related to turns using greater than, less than, or the same as.

a   An acute angle

b   An obtuse angle

c   A straight angle

Activity 2 Relating angle measures to fractional parts of a circle

The circle has *O* as its center and is divided into 360 equal parts.

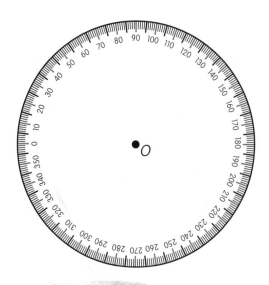

1) Draw a line segment from the center of the circle, point *O*, to the "0" mark on the circle. Label the "0°" mark point *A*.

2) Draw another line segment from the center of the circle to the "1" mark on the circle. Label this point *B*. Use a protractor to measure ∠AOB. What is the measure of ∠AOB?

3) What fraction of a full turn is ∠AOB? Explain.

4) When you measure an angle in degrees, what does the number of degrees represent?

TRY Practice relating turns to right angles and fractional parts of a circle

Fill in each blank with $\frac{1}{4}$, $\frac{1}{2}$, $\frac{3}{4}$, or 1.

1 Two right angles make up a _____-turn.

2 Four right angles is the same as _____ full turn.

3 270° is _____ of a full turn.

4 93° is between a _____-turn and a _____-turn.

5 200° is between a _____-turn and a _____-turn.

Fill in each blank with the correct fraction or angle measure.

6 1° is exactly _____ of a full turn.

7 45° is exactly _____ of a full turn.

8 30° is exactly _____ of a full turn.

9 $\frac{1}{36}$ of a full turn is exactly _____°.

10 $\frac{1}{6}$ of a full turn is exactly _____°.

INDEPENDENT PRACTICE

Use to find the measure of each angle. Then, answer each question.

1

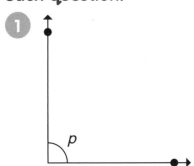

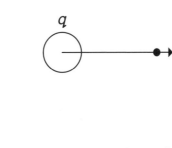

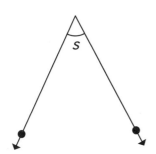

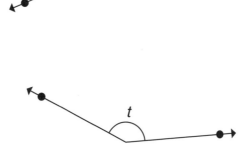

a Which angle shows a $\frac{1}{2}$-turn? ∠_____

b Which angle shows a turn greater than a $\frac{1}{4}$-turn but less than a $\frac{1}{2}$-turn? ∠_____

c Which angle has a measure of 90°? ∠_____

d Which angle shows a full turn? ∠_____

Fill in each blank with the correct fraction.

2 A straight angle is exactly _____ of a full turn.

3 90° is exactly _____ of a full turn.

4 20° is exactly _____ of a full turn.

5 100° is exactly _____ of a full turn.

Write the measure of each angle.

6 The measure of $\angle ABC$ is $\frac{3}{4}$ of a full turn.

7 The measure of $\angle LMN$ is $\frac{5}{6}$ of a full turn.

Finding Unknown Angles

Learning Objectives:
- Use addition or subtraction to find unknown angle measures.
- Solve real-world problems by finding unknown angle measures.

THINK

Emilia draws a point at the center of a semi-circular piece of paper and labels it *O*. She draws a line segment from point *O* to the edge of the paper. Two angles are formed at point *O*. One of the angles formed at point *O* is an obtuse angle. If all the angle measures are in whole degrees, what is the greatest possible measure of the other angle?

ENGAGE

1 The hour hand and minute hand are both pointing at 12. What is the angle formed when the hour hand and the minute hand are pointing in the opposite direction of each other.

2 The hour hand and minute hand are both pointing at 12. The hour hand and the minute hand are then turned in opposite directions. What angle would they have turned when they meet again?

3 The hour hand and minute hand are both pointing at 12. The hour hand is then turned 3 times as fast as the minute hand in the opposite direction. What angle would the hour hand have turned when the two hands meet?

Draw a picture to show each angle formed.

LEARN Find unknown angles

1 In the diagram below, ∠*AOC* is divided up into two non-overlapping

angles ∠*AOB* and ∠*BOC*. ∠*AOB* and ∠*BOC* share a side $\overrightarrow{OB}$.

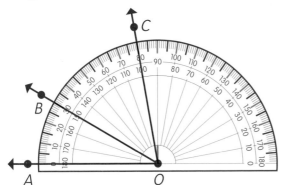

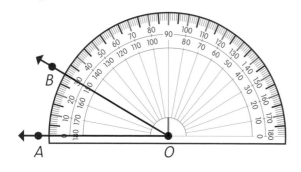

$\angle AOB = 30°$

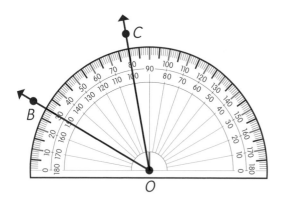

$\angle BOC = 50°$

Measure of $\angle AOB + \angle BOC = 30° + 50°$
$= 80°$

You can also see that the measure of $\angle AOC = 80°$.

So, the measure of $\angle AOC$ is the sum of the measures of $\angle AOB$ and $\angle BOC$.

$m\angle AOC = m\angle AOB + m\angle BOC$

The measures of angles that share
a side can be added.

You can write the measure
of $\angle AOC$ as $m\angle AOC$.

2 Find the measure of ∠PXR.

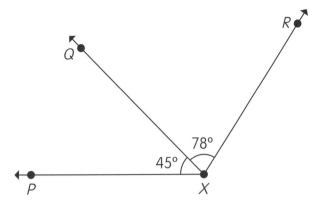

m∠PXR = m∠PXQ + m∠QXR
      = 45° + 78°
      = 123°

3 ∠ABC is a right angle. Find the measure of ∠x.

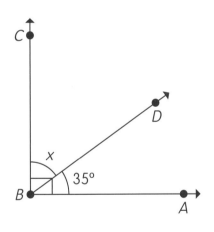

m∠x + 35° = 90°
So, m∠x = 90° − 35°
         = 55°

A right angle has a measure of 90°.

4 ∠POQ is a straight angle. Find the measure of ∠POR.

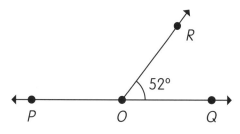

A straight angle has a measure of 180°.

m∠POR + 52° = 180°

So, m∠POR = 180° − 52°

= 128°

TRY Practice finding unknown angles

Find each unknown angle.

1 The measure of ∠XOY is 125° and the measure of ∠YOZ is 15°. Find the measure of ∠XOZ.

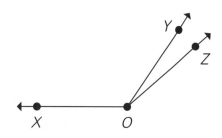

m∠XOZ = _____ ° ◯ _____ °

= _____ °

2 The measure of ∠TZV is 98°. Find the measure of ∠y.

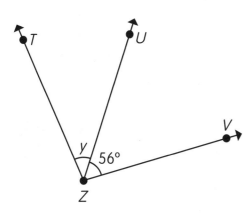

m∠y + _____° = _____°

So, m∠y = _____° ◯ _____°

= _____°

3 The measure of ∠FOG is 72°. The measure of ∠GOH is 108°. What can you say about ∠FOH? Explain.

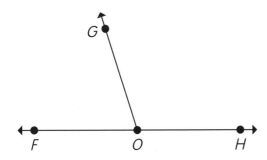

4 In each diagram, ∠COD is a straight angle.

a Find the measure of ∠b.

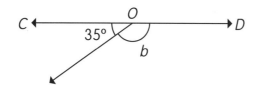

b Find the measure of ∠p.

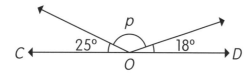

5 ABCD is a rectangle. Find the measure of ∠x.

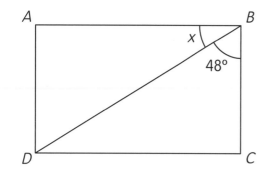

Each angle of a rectangle is a right angle.

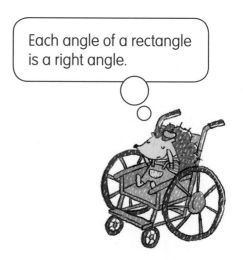

ENGAGE

Fold a square piece of paper along the diagonal. What can you say about the new angles formed in the corners? What are the measures of the new angles? How do you know?

LEARN Solve real-world problems involving unknown angles

1 Shanti makes a paper clock for her project. The clock is a circle with three hands — the hour hand, the minute hand, and the second hand.

a Find the measure of ∠AOB.

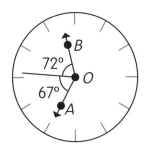

$$m\angle AOB = 67° + 72°$$
$$= 139°$$

b Shanti then turns the three hands of the clock to form new angles as shown. Find the measure of ∠x.

$$m\angle x = 155° - 123°$$
$$= 32°$$

TRY Practice solving real-world problems involving unknown angles

Find each unknown angle.

1 Vijay used a rectangular piece of cardboard and a triangular piece of cardboard to make a model of a house. The measure of ∠PTQ is 35°. What is the measure of ∠PTS?

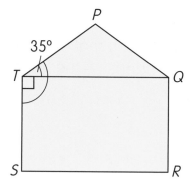

2 Ms. Mitchell has a square piece of cloth. She wants to cut the cloth as shown to make a pattern. What is the measure of ∠y?

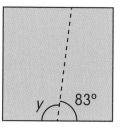

INDEPENDENT PRACTICE

These figures may not be drawn to scale.
Find the measure of each unknown angle.

1 Find the measure of ∠EPG.

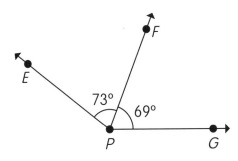

2 The measure of ∠LQN is 84°. Find the measure of ∠x.

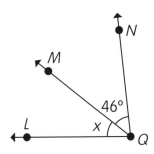

3 ∠XYZ is a straight angle. Find the measure of ∠WYZ.

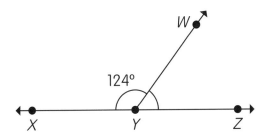

4 Silvana buys a paper fan during a carnival.
Find the measure of ∠LTN.

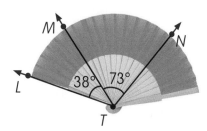

5 The diagram shows a menu. The measure of ∠XPZ is 168°.
Find the measure of ∠b.

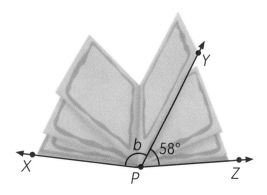

6 Mr. Hill wants to paint a rectangular wall two different colors as shown.
What is the measure of ∠g?

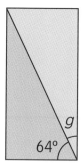

5 Drawing Perpendicular and Parallel Line Segments

Learning Objectives:
- Draw perpendicular line segments.
- Draw parallel line segments.

New Vocabulary
drawing triangle

 THINK

Draw a quadrilateral that has two pairs of parallel sides and two pairs of perpendicular sides on a square grid. Name the quadrilateral you have drawn. Can you draw a different quadrilateral with the same number of parallel sides and perpendicular sides? If yes, name the quadrilateral.

ENGAGE

Draw $\overline{AB}$. Using point B as the vertex, draw $\overline{BC}$ such that $\angle ABC$ measures 90°. How can you describe the line segments?

LEARN Draw perpendicular line segments

1 You can use a protractor to draw perpendicular line segments.

Draw a line segment that is perpendicular to $\overline{AB}$.

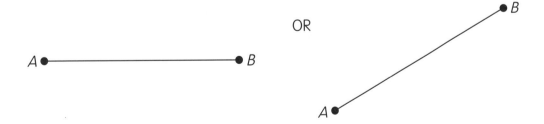

OR

STEP 1 Mark a point on $\overline{AB}$ and label it C.
Place the base line of the protractor on $\overline{AB}$.
Align the center of the base line with point C.
Use the inner or outer scale to find the 90° mark.

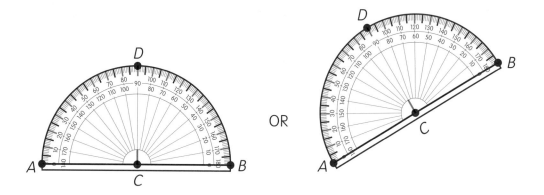

OR

STEP 2 Use a straightedge to connect point C and point D.

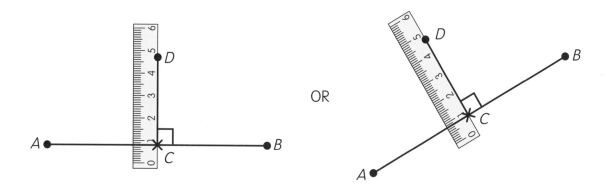

OR

$\overline{AB}$ and $\overline{CD}$ are perpendicular line segments. You can write this as $\overline{AB} \perp \overline{CD}$.

2 You can also use a drawing triangle to draw perpendicular lines.

STEP **1** Mark a point C on $\overline{AB}$.
Place the straight edge of the drawing triangle on $\overline{AB}$. Place its right-angled corner at point C. Mark a point at the third corner of the drawing triangle. Label this point D.

A drawing triangle is in the shape of a right triangle, because it has one right angle.

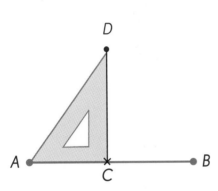

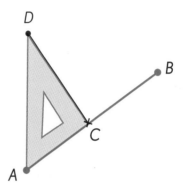

STEP **2** Connect point C and point D.

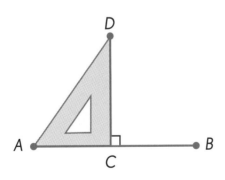

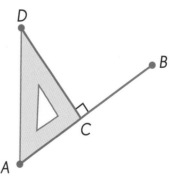

$\overline{AB}$ and $\overline{CD}$ are perpendicular line segments.
$\overline{AB} \perp \overline{CD}$

Work in pairs.

Activity 1 Drawing perpendicular line segments

① Draw a line segment in the space below. Ask your partner to mark a point near the line segment.

② **Mathematical Habit 5** Use tools strategically

Draw a line segment perpendicular to the line segment in ① through the point your partner drew.

③ Take turns to mark points and draw line segments that are perpendicular to the line segment in ① through the points.

④ Check that the line segments are perpendicular.

Activity 2   Explaining how perpendicular line segments are drawn

(1) Look at the pairs of perpendicular line segments drawn. Study how these pairs of perpendicular line segments are drawn.

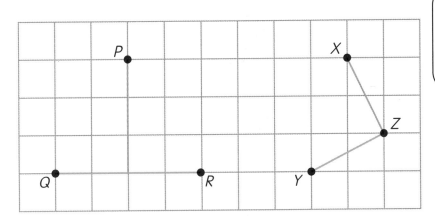

How do we know these line segments are perpendicular to one another?

(2) Draw a few more pairs of perpendicular line segments in the grid below. How do we know that they are perpendicular to each other?

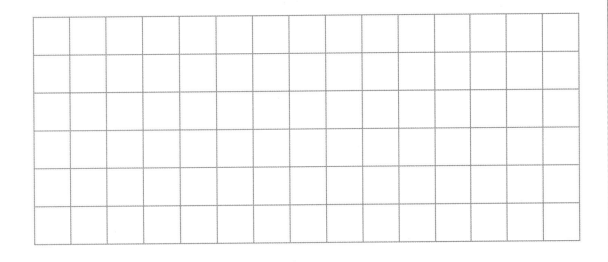

(3) Ask your partner to check that the line segments are perpendicular to each other.

For each line segment, draw a line segment perpendicular to it.

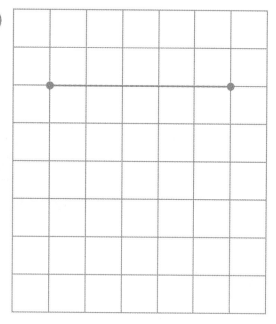

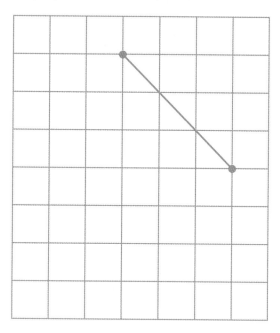

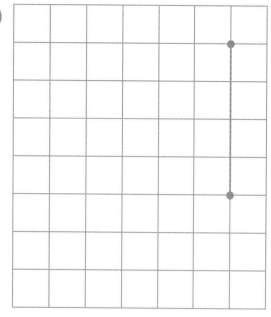

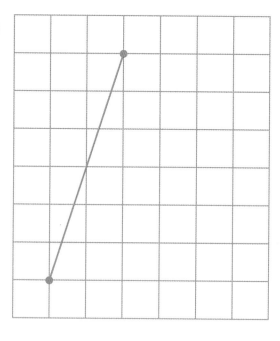

Draw a line segment perpendicular to each given line segment through point A.

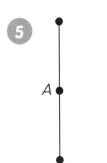

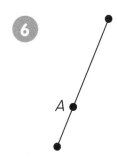

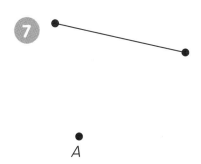

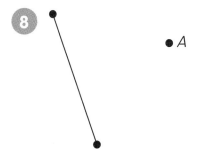

ENGAGE

Draw $\overline{AB}$ on a square grid. How can you draw $\overline{CD}$ such that $\overline{AB}$ and $\overline{CD}$ are parallel? Use a protractor to prove your lines are parallel. Share with your partner.

LEARN Draw parallel line segments

1 You can use a drawing triangle to draw parallel line segments.

STEP 1 Place a drawing triangle against $\overline{PQ}$.
Then place a straightedge at the base of the drawing triangle.

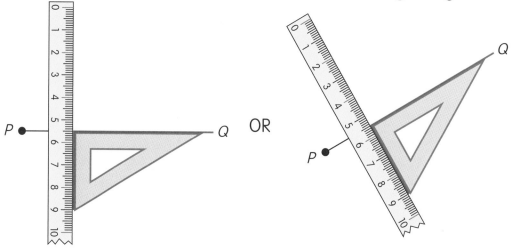

OR

STEP 2 Slide the drawing triangle along the straightedge.
Then use the edge of the drawing triangle to draw $\overline{MN}$.

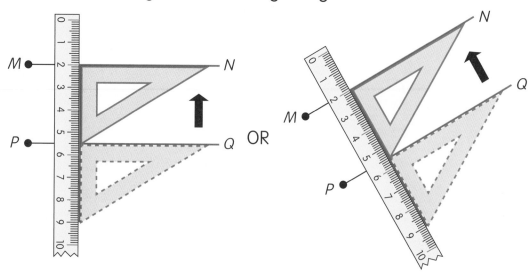

OR

$\overline{PQ}$ and $\overline{MN}$ are parallel line segments.
You can write this as $\overline{PQ} \parallel \overline{MN}$.

2 Draw a line segment parallel to $\overline{CD}$ through point R.

STEP 1 ▶ Place a drawing triangle against $\overline{CD}$. Then, place a straightedge at the base of the drawing triangle.

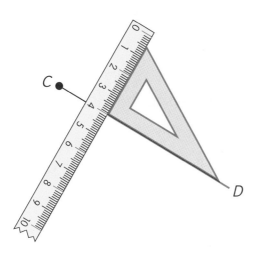

STEP 2 ▶ Slide the drawing triangle along the straightedge until the edge of the drawing triangle touches point R. Then, draw a line segment through point R and label it EF.

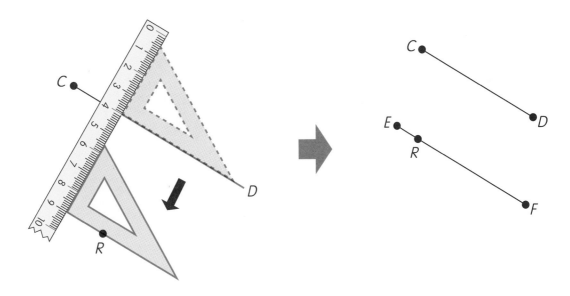

$\overline{EF}$ is parallel to $\overline{CD}$.
$\overline{EF} \parallel \overline{CD}$

Work in pairs.

Activity 1 Drawing parallel line segments

① Draw a line segment in the space below. Ask your partner to mark a point near the line segment.

② **Mathematical Habit 5** Use tools strategically
Draw a line segment parallel to the line segment in ① through the point your partner drew.

③ Take turns to mark points and draw line segments that are parallel to the line segment in ① through the points.

④ Check that the line segments are parallel.

Activity 2   Explaining how parallel line segments are drawn

1. Look at the pairs of parallel line segments drawn. Study how these pairs of parallel line segments are drawn.

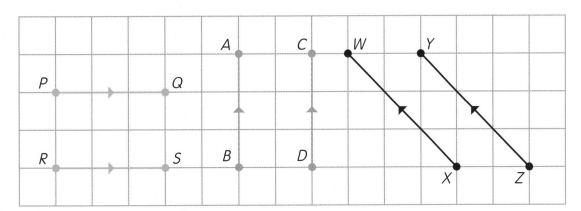

2. Draw a few more pairs of parallel line segments in the grid below. Explain why they are parallel to each other.

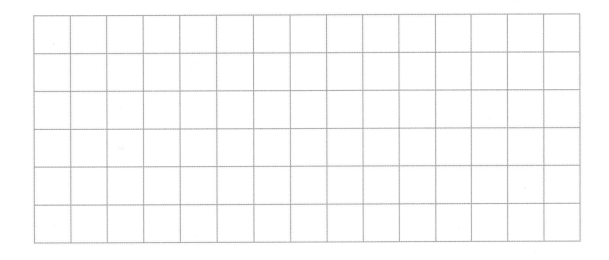

3. Ask your partner to check that the line segments are parallel to each other.

Practice drawing parallel line segments

For each line segment, draw a line segment parallel to it.

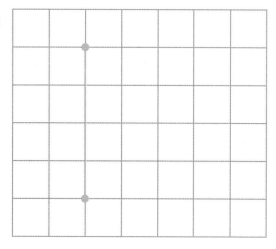

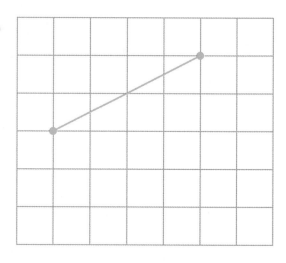

Draw a line segment parallel to each given line segment through point *B*.

B

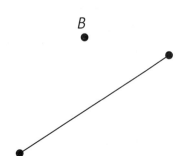

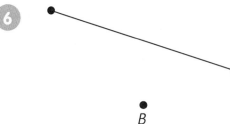

INDEPENDENT PRACTICE

Draw a line segment perpendicular to each given line segment through point _A_.

 1

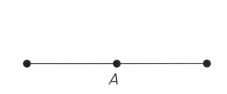

 2

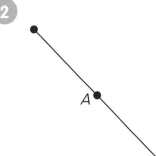

 3

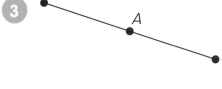

 4

Draw a line segment parallel to each given line segment through point *B*.

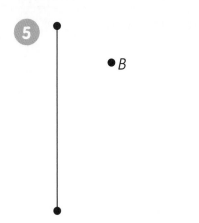

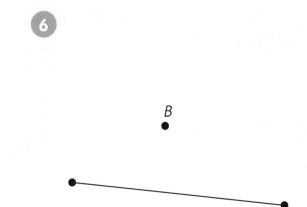

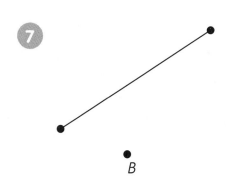

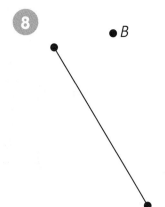

Look at the figure. Follow each direction and answer each question.

⑨ Draw a line segment perpendicular to $\overline{AB}$ and passing through point B.

⑩ Draw a line segment perpendicular to $\overline{AD}$ and passing through point D.

⑪ Extend each line segment you drew in ⑨ and ⑩ until they meet. Label this point C.

⑫ a What do you notice about the two line segments you have drawn?

_____

  b What shape did you form?

_____

⑬ Draw the line segment AC. Name the two right triangles that are formed.

_____

Complete the figure.

14 Figure A is made up of two identical squares. Complete the figure on the right to form a figure identical to the figure A.

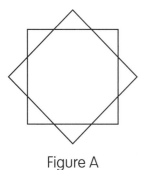

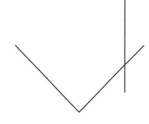

Figure A

Look at the figure. Follow each direction and answer each question.

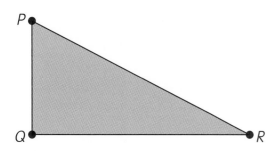

15 Draw a line segment parallel to $\overline{QR}$ and passing through point P.

16 Draw a line segment parallel to $\overline{PQ}$ and passing through point R.

17 Extend each line segment in **15** and **16** until they meet.
What do you notice about the two line segments you have drawn?

_____

18 What do you notice about the figure you have drawn?

_____

1 **Mathematical Habit 2** Use mathematical reasoning

The steps for measuring these angles are not in order.
Arrange the steps in order by using 1, 2, or 3 in each box.

a   Obtuse angle

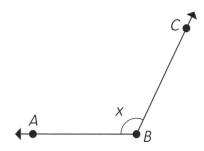

Step _____ Place the center of the base line of the protractor at vertex *B* of the angle.

Step _____ Place the base line of the protractor on ray *BA*.

Step _____ Read the outer scale at the point where ray *BC* crosses it. The reading is 116°. So, the angle measure is 116°.

b   Acute angle

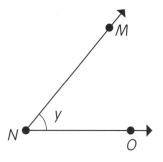

Step _____ Read the inner scale at the point where ray *NM* crosses it. The reading is 50°. So, the angle measure is 50°.

Step _____ Place the base line of the protractor on ray *NO*.

Step _____ Place the center of the base line of the protractor at vertex *N* of the angle.

c   Compare the measures of the two angles in **a** and **b**.
Use < and > in your answers.

1 **Mathematical Habit 1** Persevere in solving problems
An acute angle is smaller than 90°. ∠PQR is an acute angle. How many acute angles are there altogether in the following figure?

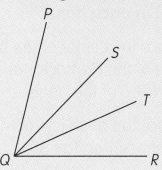

2 **Mathematical Habit 8** Look for patterns
How many right angles does the hour hand of a clock move from 8 A.M. today to 2 A.M. tomorrow?

3 **Mathematical Habit 4** Use mathematical models
A square piece of paper is folded as shown.
Find ∠p.

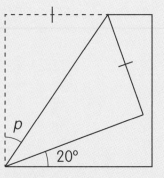

CHAPTER WRAP-UP

 How can you measure and draw angles? How can you draw perpendicular and parallel line segments?

Angles

Naming Angles

Name the angle at vertex B as $\angle ABC$, $\angle CBA$, or $\angle x$.

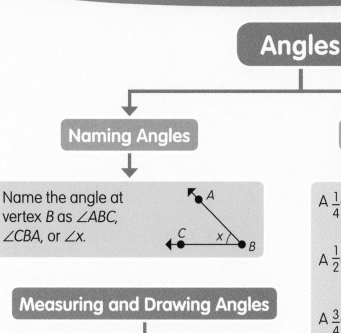

Measuring and Drawing Angles

You can use a protractor to measure and draw angles.
The measure of $\angle ABC$ is 45°.

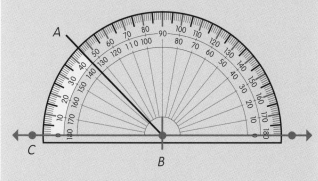

The measure of $\angle DEF$ is 145°.

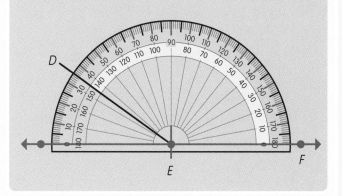

Relating Turns and Right Angles

A $\frac{1}{4}$-turn is one right angle or 90°.

A $\frac{1}{2}$-turn is two right angles or 180°.

A $\frac{3}{4}$-turn is three right angles or 270°.

One full turn is four right angles or 360°.

Relating Turns and Right Angles

The measures of angles that share a side can be added.

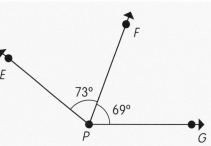

$m\angle EPF + m\angle FPG$
$= m\angle EPG$

You can use addition or subtraction to find unknown angles.

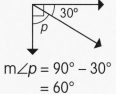 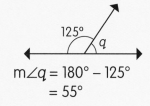

$m\angle p = 90° - 30°$
$ = 60°$

$m\angle q = 180° - 125°$
$ = 55°$

Draw a line segment perpendicular to a given line segment
• through a point on the given line segment (use a drawing triangle and protractor).
• through a point not on the given line segment (use a drawing triangle).

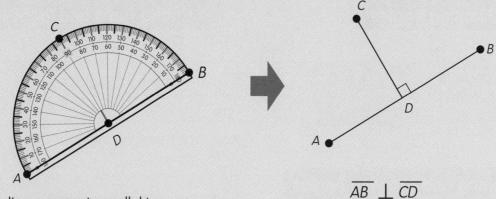

$$\overline{AB} \perp \overline{CD}$$

Draw a line segment parallel to
• a given line segment.
• a given line segment and passing through a given point.

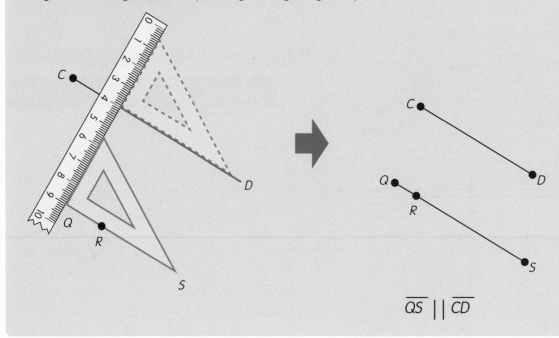

$$\overline{QS} \parallel \overline{CD}$$

Name: _____ Date: _____

Name each angle in the triangle.

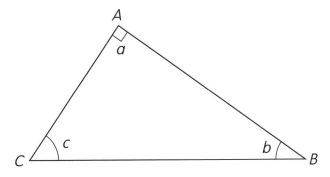

1 ∠a = _____

2 ∠b = _____

3 ∠c = _____

Name each correct angle.

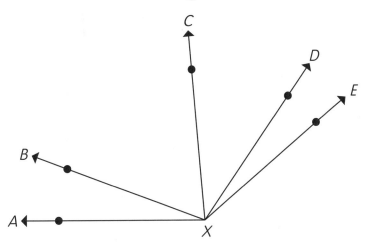

4 Name the angle that measures 85°. _____

5 Name the angle that measures 120°. _____

Use a protractor to measure each angle in the following figure.

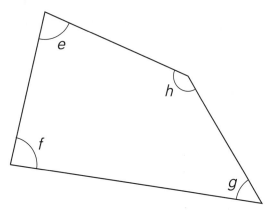

6　Measure of ∠e = _____

7　Measure of ∠f = _____

8　Measure of ∠g = _____

9　Measure of ∠h = _____

Draw an angle that has each of the following measures.

10　64°

11　178°

Fill in each blank.

12 A $\frac{3}{4}$-turn is _____°.

13 90° is a _____ -turn

14 One full turn is _____°.

15 30° is exactly _____ of a full turn.

These figures may not be drawn to scale. Find each unknown angle.

16 In the diagram, ∠AOC is 110°. Find the measure of ∠BOC.

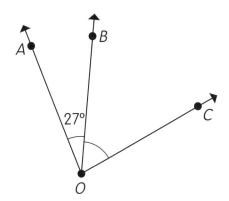

17 ∠WOZ is a straight angle. Find the measure of ∠XOY.

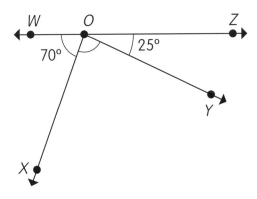

Solve.

18 Amirah folded a square paper in half to form a right triangle, as shown. What is the measure of ∠BDC?

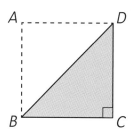

19 Look at the clock face. The hour hand and the minute hand form an angle measure of 130°. The minute hand and the second hand form an angle measure of 42°. Find the measure of the marked angle formed by the hour hand and the second hand.

20 Draw a line segment perpendicular to $\overline{XY}$ through point Y.

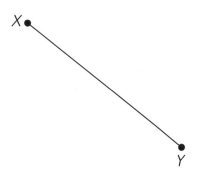

Draw a line segment parallel to $\overline{QR}$ through point P.

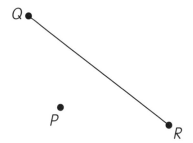

Assessment Prep

Answer each question.

22 Which statement about turns and angle measures is true?

Ⓐ A full turn is 360 right angles.

Ⓑ A straight angle is the same as a $\frac{1}{4}$-turn.

Ⓒ An angle that turns through $\frac{1}{360}$ of a full turn has a measure of 1°.

Ⓓ An angle that turns through $\frac{3}{4}$ of a full turn has a measure of 180°.

23 Which angle has a measure of 85°?

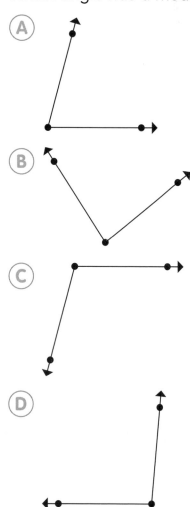

Ⓐ Ⓑ Ⓒ Ⓓ

24 The measure of ∠AOB is 112°. Find the measure of ∠DOC.
Write your answer and your work in the space below.

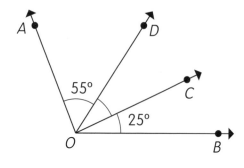

Creating Designs

1 Evan and Jack are studying an art piece. In the art piece, two rays form an angle as shown below. They each measure the angle.

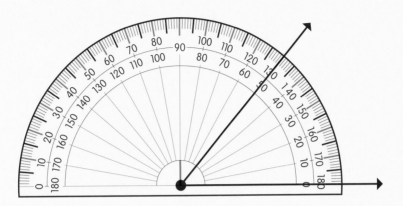

a Evan says the measure of the angle is 50°, but Jack says it is 130°. Who is correct, Evan or Jack?
Explain your answer.

b Evan says the angle is an acute angle. Jack says the angle is less than a straight angle. Explain whether their statements are correct.

2 John draws a simple map to show the route he takes to walk to the library. One of the directions on his map is to make a $\frac{1}{2}$-turn, which is also the same as 180°. After the $\frac{1}{2}$-turn, he hikes for another 100 meters before making a 270° turn. Relate the 270° turn to a fraction of a full turn.

3 A designer drew a model of some of the pathways in an apartment complex.
Use your understanding of perpendicular and parallel lines to add the pathways that are missing to the drawing.

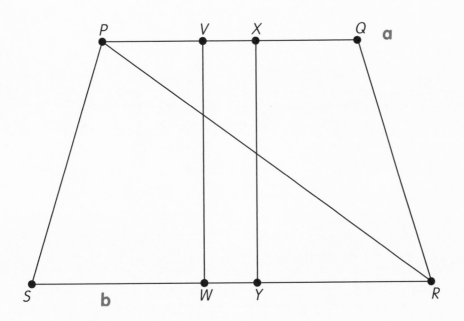

a Draw a pathway that is parallel to *PR* through point *Q*.
b Draw a pathway that is parallel to *VW*, perpendicular to *SR*, and goes through point *P*.

4 Draw inside the outline to design a shirt that has parallel stripes.

Rubric

Point(s)	Level	My Performance
7–8	4	• Most of my answers are correct. • I showed complete understanding of what I have learned. • I used the correct strategies to solve the problems. • I explained my answers and mathematical thinking clearly and completely.
5–6.5	3	• Some of my answers are correct. • I showed some understanding of what I have learned. • I used some correct strategies to solve the problems. • I explained my answers and mathematical thinking clearly.
3–4.5	2	• A few of my answers are correct. • I showed little understanding of what I have learned. • I used a few correct strategies to solve the problems. • I explained some of my answers and mathematical thinking clearly.
0–2.5	1	• A few of my answers are correct. • I showed little or no understanding of what I have learned. • I used a few strategies to solve the problems. • I did not explain my answers and mathematical thinking clearly.

Teacher's Comments

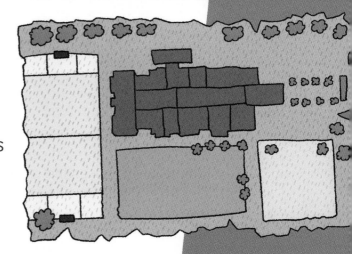

Treasure Hunt

A treasure hunt is a very popular game played among children at parties. Players are given clues to solve along with a treasure map for guidance.

Task

Create a Treasure Hunt

1 Decide on an item, or some items, to be the treasure. Hide the treasure somewhere within the school grounds.

2 Draw a simple map of the school grounds. Make sure you can identify where the treasure is hidden on the map.

3 Choose at least four points on the map (other than the final treasure point) where you will hide the clues. Each clue will lead players to the next point, and eventually, to the treasure.

4 Use your understanding of angles, turns, perpendicular lines, and parallel lines to come up with the clues. For example:

From the hall, make a $\frac{1}{4}$-turn to the right and walk about 20 steps. Walk 15 steps parallel to the field, then turn about 45° to the left.

Polygons and Symmetry

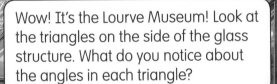

Wow! It's the Lourve Museum! Look at the triangles on the side of the glass structure. What do you notice about the angles in each triangle?

What do you notice about the right and left sides of its building?

How do you sort and classify polygons?
How can you identify symmetric shapes and patterns?

RECALL PRIOR KNOWLEDGE

Name: ______________________ Date: ____________

Identifying polygons

Name of Polygon	Number of Sides	Number of Vertices	Number of Angles
Triangle 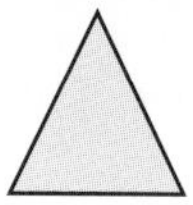	3	3	3
Rectangle	4	4	4
Square	4	4	4
Parallelogram 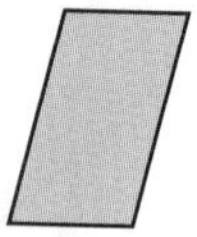	4	4	4
Trapezoid 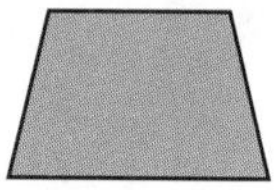	4	4	4
Rhombus 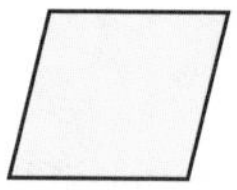	4	4	4
Pentagon 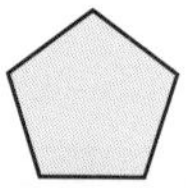	5	5	5
Hexagon 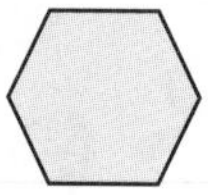	6	6	6

▶ Quick Check

Identify each polygon.

1 It has 3 sides and 3 vertices. _____

2 It has 4 sides and 4 vertices. _____

3 It has 5 sides and 5 angles. _____

Identifying quadrilaterals

A quadrilateral is a polygon with four sides and four angles.

Name of Quadrilateral	Characteristics of Quadrilateral
Rectangle	• Opposite sides are parallel. • Opposite sides are of equal length. • All four angles are right angles.
Square	• Opposite sides are parallel. • All sides are of equal length. • All four angles are right angles.
Parallelogram	• Opposite sides are parallel. • Opposite sides are of equal length. • There are four angles.
Rhombus	• Opposite sides are parallel. • All sides are of equal length. • There are four angles.
Trapezoid	• Only one pair of opposite sides are parallel. • There are four angles.

▶ **Quick Check**

Fill in each blank.

4️⃣ The opposite _____ of a parallelogram are parallel.

5️⃣ Each angle of a _____ and a _____ is a right angle.

6️⃣ The four sides of a square are of _____ length.

7️⃣ A trapezoid has only one pair of opposite sides that are _____.

8️⃣ The four sides of a rhombus are of _____ length.

Combining plane shapes to form other plane shapes

Two squares can be combined to form a rectangle.

▶ **Quick Check**

Tick (✔) the box below the correct shape.

9️⃣ Which shape do you get when you combine two  ?

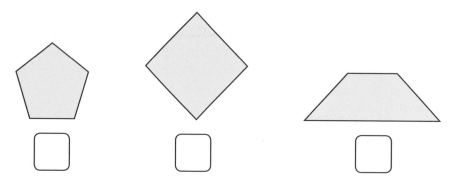

Classifying Triangles

Learning Objective:
- Classify triangles by their angle measures.

New Vocabulary
obtuse triangle
acute triangle

THINK

Anna joins two identical triangles to form a rectangle. Which triangles did she use? Explain. Using different identical triangles, draw to show different quadrilaterals you can form.

ENGAGE

Look at the angles in each triangle.

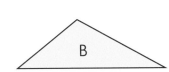

Use  to find out whether each angle is a right angle, smaller than a right angle, or larger than a right angle. What do you notice about the three angles in each triangle? Share your ideas with your partner.

LEARN Classify triangles by their angle measures

1 In Triangle *PQR*, ∠*QRP* is a right angle.
Triangle *PQR* is a right triangle.
A right triangle has one right angle.

Use to mark the right angle.

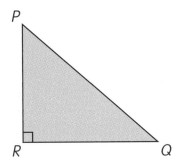

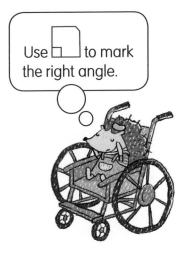

2 In Triangle *STU*, the measure of ∠*UST* is greater than 90°.
Triangle *STU* is an obtuse triangle.
An obtuse triangle has one obtuse angle.

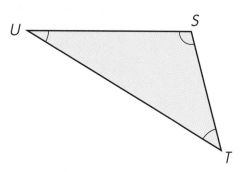

3 In Triangle *XYZ*, the measures of all the angles are less than 90°.
Triangle *XYZ* is an acute triangle.
An acute triangle has three acute angles.

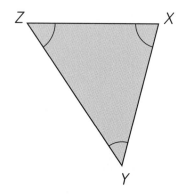

 Math Talk

Cameron says it is impossible to draw a triangle with one obtuse angle,
one right angle, and one acute angle. Do you agree? Explain.

Hands-on Activity ▶ Classifying acute, obtuse, and right triangles

Work in pairs.

(1) Use 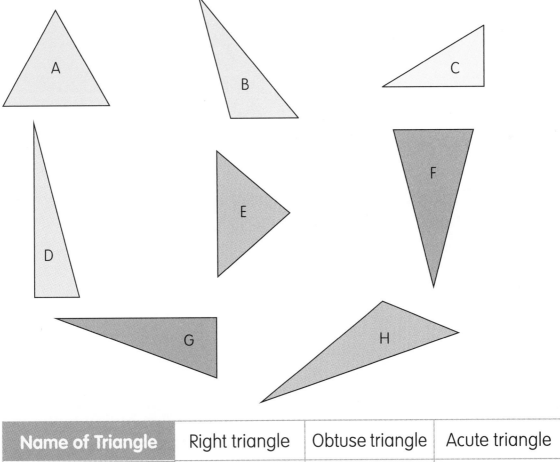 to measure the angles in each triangle below.

(2) Sort the triangles by their angle measures and complete the table below. Write the letter of each triangle in the correct group.

Name of Triangle	Right triangle	Obtuse triangle	Acute triangle
Triangles			

(3) Explain how you have sorted the triangles.

TRY Practice classifying triangles by their angle measures

Which of these triangles is right, obtuse, or acute?
Use 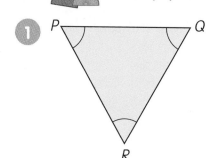 to help you.

1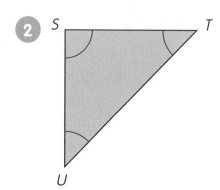

Measure of ∠RPQ = _____°

Measure of ∠PQR = _____°

Measure of ∠QRP = _____°

Triangle *PQR* is a/an _____ triangle.

2

Measure of ∠UST = _____°

Measure of ∠STU = _____°

Measure of ∠TUS = _____°

Triangle *STU* is a/an _____ triangle.

3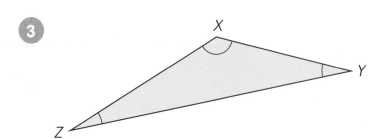

Measure of ∠ZXY = _____°

Measure of ∠XYZ = _____°

Measure of ∠YZX = _____°

Triangle *XYZ* is a/an _____ triangle.

INDEPENDENT PRACTICE

Classify each triangle as right, obtuse, or acute.
Use to help you.

1

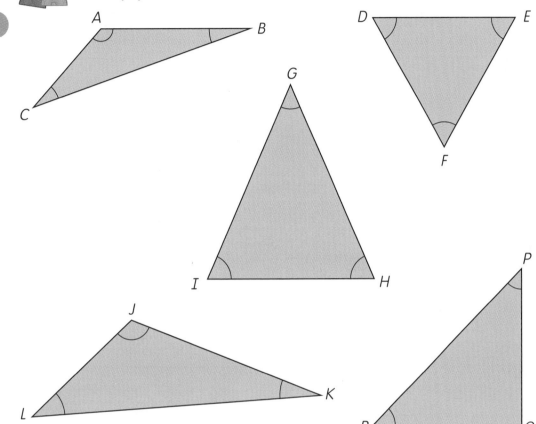

Name of Triangle	Triangles
Right triangle	
Obtuse triangle	
Acute triangle	

Circle the triangle that does not belong in each set. Explain.

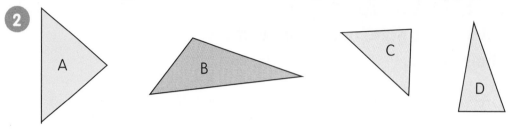

2

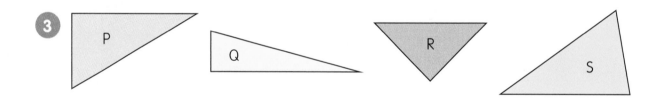

3

2 Classifying Polygons

Learning Objective:
- Classify quadrilaterals by their properties.

THINK

Draw straight lines to cut the hexagon into shapes.
Draw and write down the different shapes you can cut.

ENGAGE

Look at the square, the right triangle, and the rhombus.

In what ways are they alike? In what ways are they different?
Use a ruler and a protractor to help you explain your answers.

LEARN Classify polygons

1 Jonathan and Aika each cut out the following polygons.

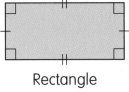

Rectangle

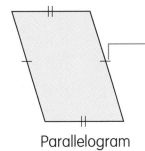
Parallelogram

> The tick marks tell us which line segments in the polygon have the same length.

Trapezoid

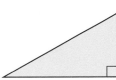
Right Triangle

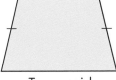
Trapezoid

Jonathan sorts the polygons into two groups.

At Least One Pair of Equal Sides	No Equal Sides

Aika sorts the polygons in a different way.

At Least One Pair of Perpendicular Sides	No Perpendicular Sides

Math Talk

What is another way to sort the polygons?

Work in pairs.

Your teacher will give you some cut-outs of quadrilaterals.

(1) Complete the table below.

You may use and a ruler to help you.

Property	Quadrilateral				
	A	B	C	D	E
It has four sides.					
All of its sides are equal.					
All of its angles are right angles.					
Its opposite sides are equal.					
It has exactly one pair of parallel sides.					
It has exactly two pairs of parallel sides.					

(2) Fill in each blank using the information in the table.

a Figure _____ is a rectangle but **not** a square.

b Figure _____ is a rhombus but **not** a square.

c Figure _____ is a parallelogram but **not** a rectangle.

d Figure _____ is a trapezoid.

3. Sort the quadrilaterals into two groups. Name each group and paste each quadrilateral cut-out in the correct group.

TRY Practice classifying polygons

Sort the polygons into two groups. Write the letter of each polygon in the correct group.

1

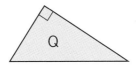
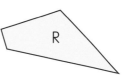
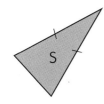
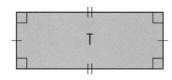

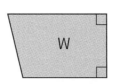

At Least One Pair of Parallel Lines	No Parallel Lines

Sort the polygons in ① in another way. Write the letter of each polygon in the correct group.

2

Quadrilateral	Not a Quadrilateral

The polygons have been sorted into two groups.
Name each group to describe how the polygons have been sorted.

A, C, D, F	B, E

Sort the polygons in ③ in another way.

④

Mathematical Habit ⑥ **Use precise mathematical language**

① Describe a rectangle and a square using the words perpendicular, parallel, and angles.

② List the similarities between a square and a rectangle.

③ Discuss how a square is related to a rectangle.

© 2020 Marshall Cavendish Education Pte Ltd

INDEPENDENT PRACTICE

Fill in each blank.

1. A _____ triangle and a rectangle each have at least

    one _____ angle.

2. A square has four equal sides. What is another polygon with four

    equal sides? _____

3. A rectangle has two pairs of parallel sides. Name two other quadrilaterals
    that have two pairs of parallel sides.

    _____

Sort the polygons into two groups. Write the letter of each polygon in the correct group.

4.

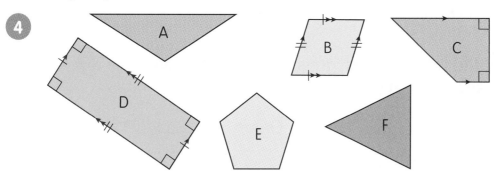

At Least One Obtuse Angle	No Obtuse Angle

Angel sorted some polygons into two groups.
Name each group to describe how Angel sorted the polygons.

5

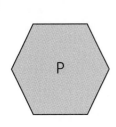
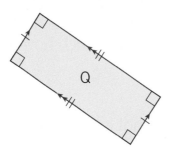
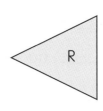

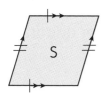
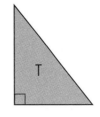
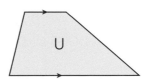

Group A:	Group B:
_____	_____
P, R, S, U	Q, T

Look at each of the following polygons. Decide which group in **5** each polygon belongs to. Explain your reasoning.

6

Group _____

Reason: _____

_____

7

Group _____

Reason: _____

_____

3 Symmetric Shapes and Lines of Symmetry

Learning Objectives:
- Identify symmetric shapes.
- Identify a line of symmetry of a figure.
- Draw lines of symmetry of a figure.

> **New Vocabulary**
> line of symmetry
> symmetric shape

THINK

A symmetric shape is drawn on a piece of paper and folded along its line of symmetry as shown. What is the shape?

ENGAGE

Look at the two shapes.

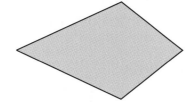

For each shape,

a draw line segments joining any two vertices (each line segment should divide the shape into two parts).

b fold along each line segment you drew to check if the two parts of the shape fit exactly onto each other.

c use a different color to go over each line segment that divides the shapes into two parts that fit exactly onto each other.

LEARN Identify symmetric shapes

1 Fold each shape along the dotted line.

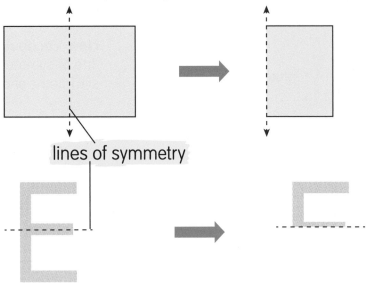

lines of symmetry

The shapes above are symmetric shapes.
The two parts in each shape match each other exactly.

2 The following are not symmetric shapes.

Why are the above not symmetric shapes?

Hands-on Activity Identifying symmetric shapes

Work in pairs.

Your teacher will give you some shapes.

(1) Fold each shape to check if it is a symmetric shape.

(2) Identify the shapes that are symmetric and complete the table. Draw the shapes under the correct group.

Symmetric Shapes	Non-Symmetric Shapes

(3) Take turns explaining to each other why each figure is symmetric or non-symmetric.

TRY Practice identifying symmetric shapes

Check (✔) the box below each symmetric shape.

(1)

Circle the letter below each symmetric shape.

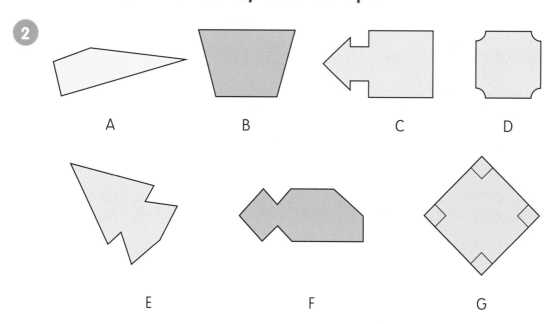

2

A   B   C   D

E   F   G

ENGAGE

Use dot paper to make a pentagon. Is it possible to make another pentagon next to the first to create a new symmetric figure? Use a drawing to justify your reasoning.

LEARN Identify and draw lines of symmetry

1 Fold the rectangle along the dotted line as shown.

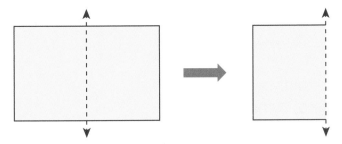

The two halves match exactly.
They are reflections of each other.

The dotted line is a line of symmetry of the rectangle.

The two halves match exactly.
They are reflections of each other.

The dotted line is another line of symmetry of the rectangle.

A symmetric shape can have more than one line of symmetry.

2 Now, fold the rectangle along the dotted line as shown.

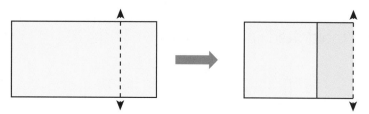

The two parts do not match exactly.
So, the dotted line is not a line of symmetry.

Fold the rectangle along the dotted line as shown.

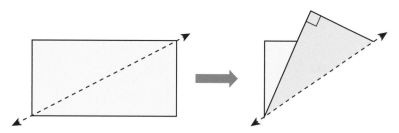

The two parts are equal, but they do not match exactly.
So, the dotted line is also not a line of symmetry.

3 Fold the square along the dotted line as shown.

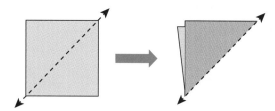

How many lines of symmetry does a square have? Draw them on the square.

The dotted line is a line of symmetry of the square.

Activity 1   Looking for symmetric shapes

Work in groups.

(1) Look for examples of symmetric shapes around the school.

(2) Take pictures of the symmetric shapes that you see.

(3) Discuss among your group how each figure is symmetric.

(4) Identify and draw a line of symmetry for each shape.

(5) Share what your group has found with other groups.

Activity 2   Finding lines of symmetry

Work in pairs.

Your teacher will give you some shapes.

(1) Select a dotted line that you think is a line of symmetry for each shape.

(2) Cut out each shape and fold along the chosen dotted line to check your answer in (1).

(3) For each symmetric shape, place a mirror along the line of symmetry. What do you notice?

TRY Practice identifying and drawing lines of symmetry

Fill in each blank. The first one has been done for you.

1. The dotted line divides each hexagon into two equal parts.
   Trace out each shape with the dotted line onto a piece of paper.

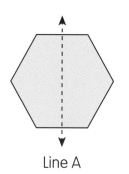

Line A

Fold a copy of the hexagon along Line A.

The two parts _____match_____ each other exactly.

Line A is ___a line of symmetry___.

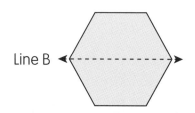

Line B

Fold a copy of the hexagon along Line B.

The two parts _____ each other exactly.

Line B is _____.

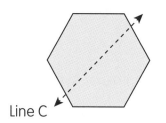

Line C

Fold a copy of the hexagon along Line C.

The two parts _____ each other exactly.

Line C is _____.

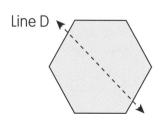

Line D

Fold a copy of the hexagon along Line D.

The two parts _____ each other exactly.

Line D is _____.

Write Yes or No in each blank.

2 Is the dotted line in each shape a line of symmetry?
If the answer is No, draw a line of symmetry for that figure.

a

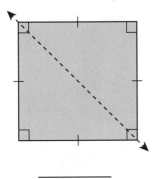

_____

b

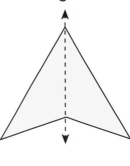

_____

c

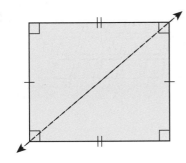

_____

d

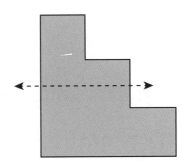

_____

e

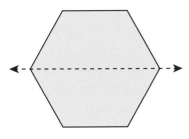

_____

f

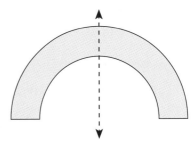

_____

MATCH THE LINES OF SYMMETRY!

What you need:

Players: 3
Materials: Alphabet cards

What to do:

1 Shuffle the cards and arrange them facedown on the table.

2 Players take turns to turn over two cards at a time. If the two cards show letters that have the same number of lines of symmetry, the player keeps the cards. If the two cards do not match, the player turns over the cards and the next player takes his or her turn.

Who is the winner?

The player with the most number of cards in the end wins!

INDEPENDENT PRACTICE

Identify the line(s) of symmetry in each figure.

1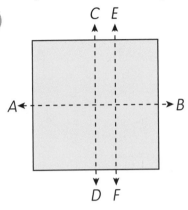

_____

2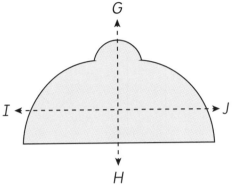

_____

3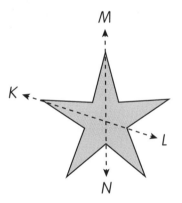

_____

4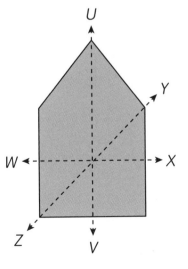

_____

5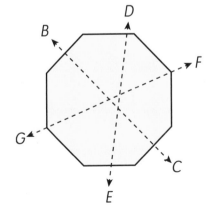

_____

6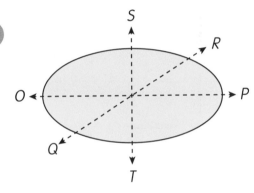

_____

Circle the letter below each symmetric shape.
Draw all the lines of symmetry of each symmetric shape.

7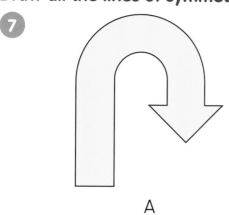

A

8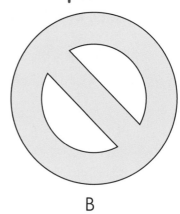

B

9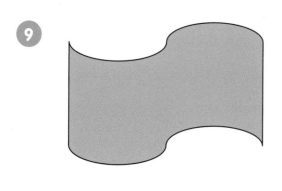

C

10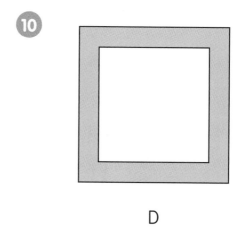

D

11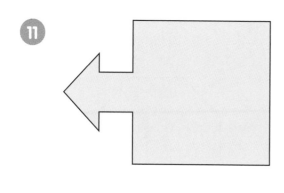

E

12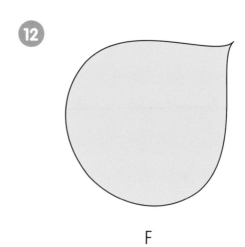

F

Making Symmetric Shapes and Patterns

Learning Objective:
• Complete a symmetric shape or pattern.

New Vocabulary
symmetric pattern

**THINK**

The pattern shown is not symmetric. Shade 3 more squares to make it a symmetric pattern. Draw the line of symmetry.

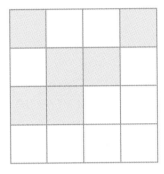

ENGAGE

Fold a piece of paper into half and cut out a shape from the folded paper.
You must start and end the cut at the folded side as shown.

Example:

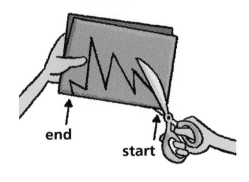

end

start

Unfold the shape you cut out. Draw a dotted line down the fold line. Explain to your partner why the shape is a symmetric shape.

LEARN Make symmetric shapes and patterns

1 You can complete symmetric shapes on square grid paper.

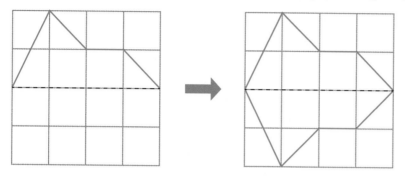

2 You can create symmetric patterns on square grid paper.

a

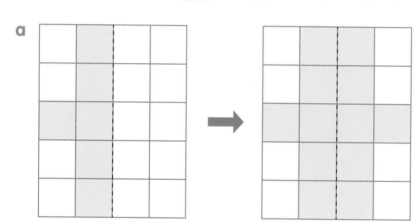

b

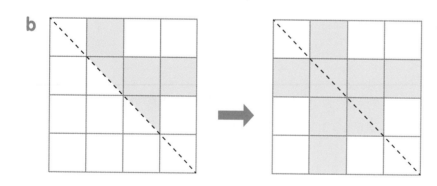

Work in pairs.

Activity 1   **Making symmetric shapes**

Your teacher will give you four small pieces of colored paper.

(1) Fold a piece of paper and cut out a symmetric figure.

(2) Draw the line of symmetry.

(3) Make four sets of the shape.

(4) Paste the shapes below to make a pattern.

Example

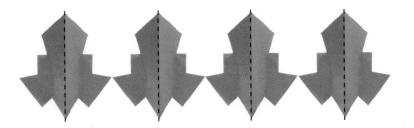

Activity 2 Making symmetric patterns

(1) Divide each square grid paper into half by drawing a vertical, horizontal, or diagonal dotted line.

(2) Color some squares on each grid to create three different symmetric patterns with the dotted line as a line of symmetry.
You may color ▨ or ◺.

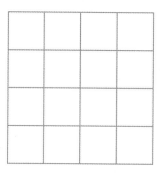

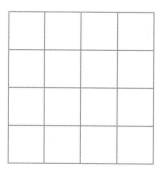

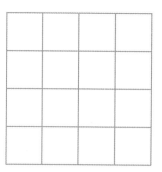

TRY Practice making symmetric shapes and patterns

Each figure shows half of a symmetric shape. The dotted line is a line of symmetry. Complete each symmetric figure.

1
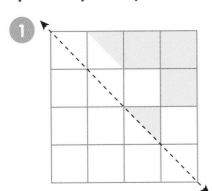

2
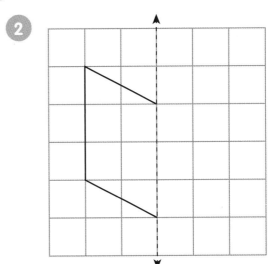

3
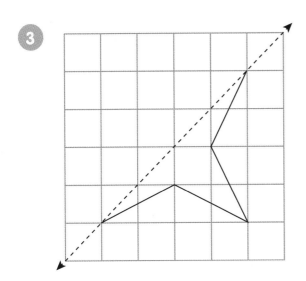

4
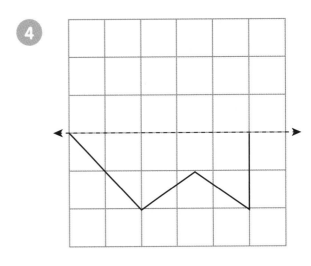

Each figure shows half of a symmetric pattern. The dotted line is a line of symmetry. Shade the squares to form a symmetric pattern about the given line of symmetry.

 5

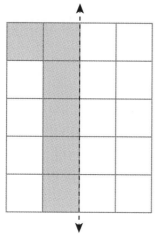

6

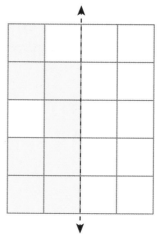

7

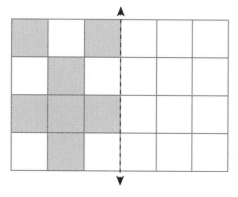

8

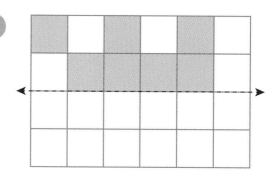

9

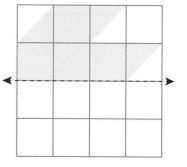

10

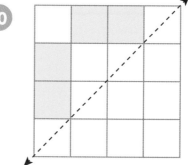

INDEPENDENT PRACTICE

Complete each symmetric shape with the dotted line as a line of symmetry.

 1

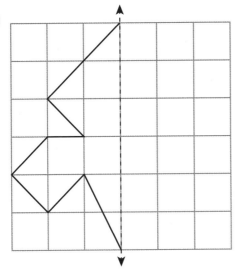

2

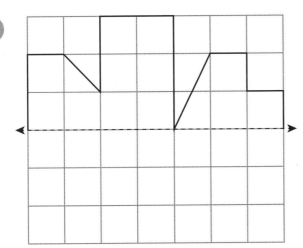

3

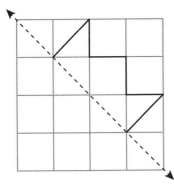

Each figure shows half of a symmetric pattern. The dotted line is a line of symmetry. Shade the squares to form a symmetric pattern about the given line of symmetry.

④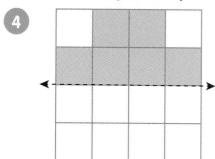

⑤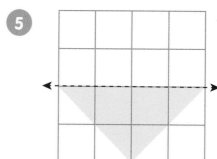

⑥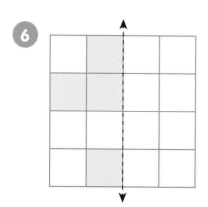

⑦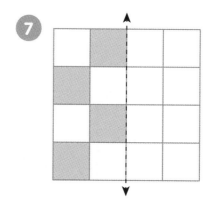

⑧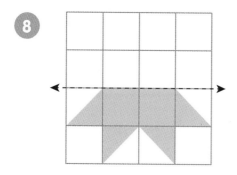

⑨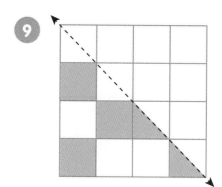

1 **Mathematical Habit 6** **Use precise mathematical language**
Explain why all squares are rectangles, but not all rectangles
are squares.

Explain how rectangles are related to parallelograms.

2 **Mathematical Habit 2** Use mathematical reasoning

a Is the following quadrilateral a symmetric shape? Explain your answer.

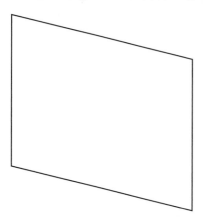

b How would you check for symmetry in a figure?

1 **Mathematical Habit 5** Use tools strategically

The trapezoid is made up of three right triangles. Draw lines to divide the trapezoid into the three triangles.

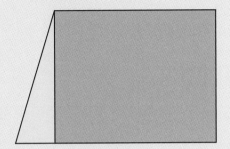

2 **Mathematical Habit 2** Use mathematical reasoning

Do the shaded squares form a symmetric pattern? Explain.

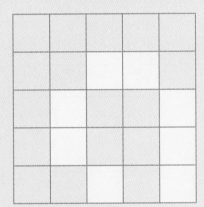

3 **Mathematical Habit 2** Use mathematical reasoning

Zane sorted some polygons into two groups as shown.
One of the polygons is in the wrong group. Circle the polygon that is in the wrong group. Explain your answer.
Then, name each group.

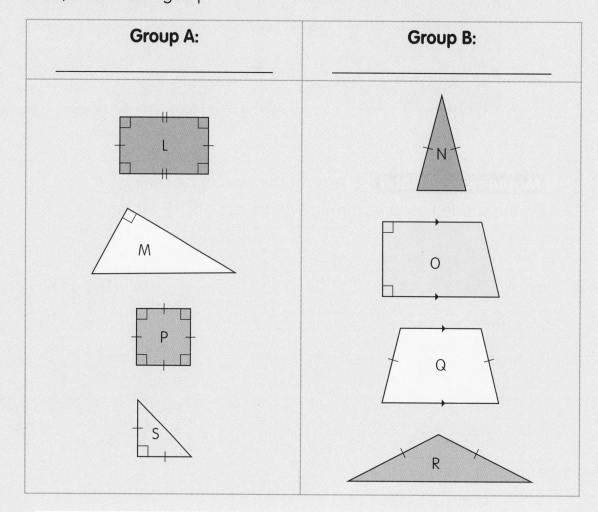

Group A:	Group B:
_____	_____

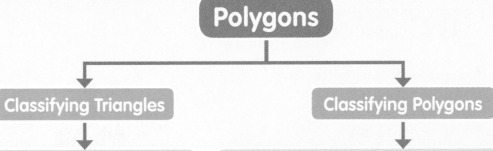

? How do you sort and classify polygons? How can you identify symmetric shapes and patterns?

Polygons

Classifying Triangles

You can classify triangles by their angle measures.
A right triangle has one right angle.

An acute triangle has three acute angles.

An obtuse triangle has one obtuse angle.

Classifying Polygons

You can classify polygons in different ways. Example:

At least one pair of parallel sides	No parallel sides

At least one right angle	No right angles

Symmetry

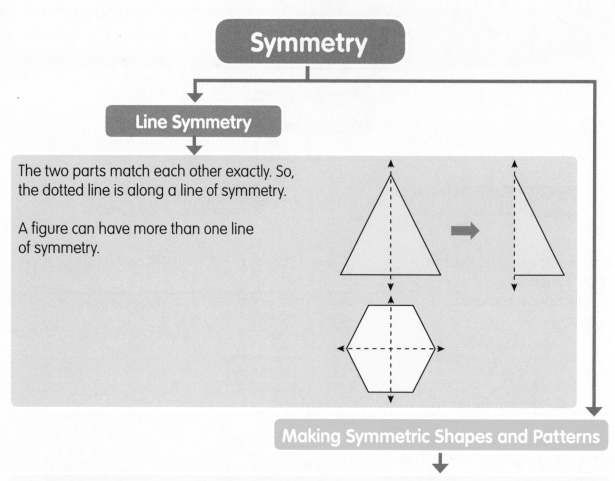

Line Symmetry

The two parts match each other exactly. So, the dotted line is along a line of symmetry.

A figure can have more than one line of symmetry.

Making Symmetric Shapes and Patterns

To complete a symmetric shape or pattern given a line of symmetry, and half of the shape or pattern.

Symmetric shape

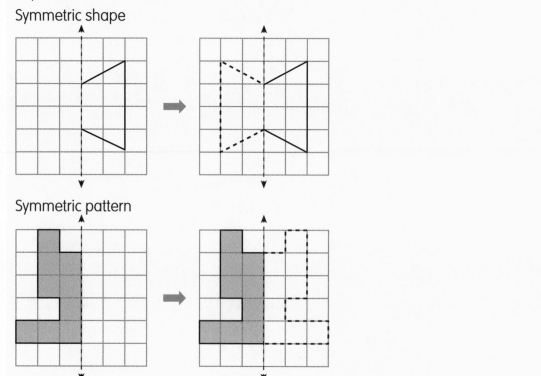

Symmetric pattern

To create symmetric patterns on grid paper.

Name: _____ Date: _____

Classify each triangle as right, obtuse, or acute.
Use to help you.

1

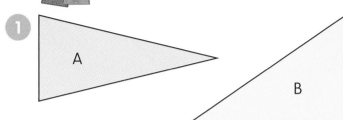

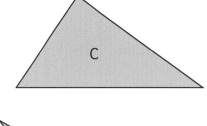

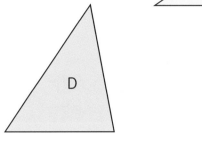

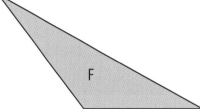

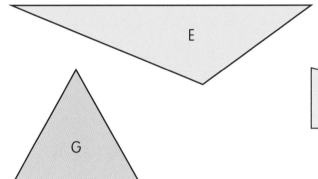

Name of Triangle	Right triangle	Obtuse triangle	Acute triangle
Triangles			

Sort the polygons into two groups. Write the letter of each polygon in the correct group.

2

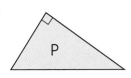

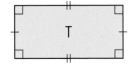 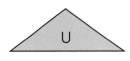

At Least One Pair of Parallel Lines	No Parallel Lines

Sort the polygons in 2 in another way. Write the letter of each polygon in the correct group.

3

At Least One Pair of Perpendicular Sides	No Perpendicular Sides

Tick (✔) each symmetric shape. Draw all the lines of symmetry for each symmetric shape.

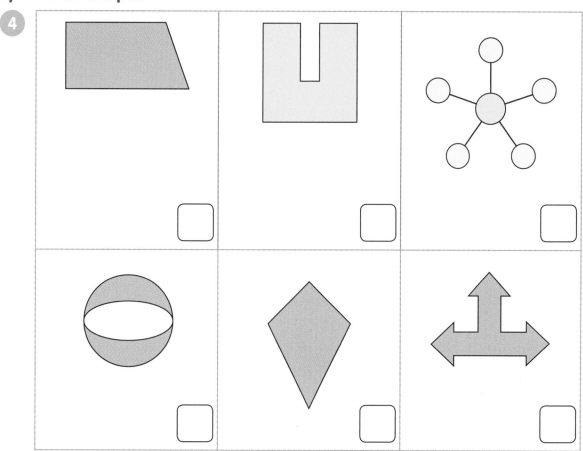

Which of the dotted lines are lines of symmetry?
Write Yes or No in each blank.

5 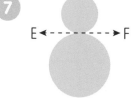 A / B _____

6 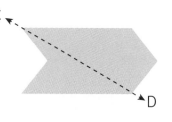 C / D _____

7 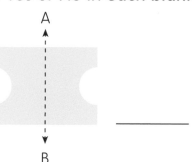 E / F _____

8 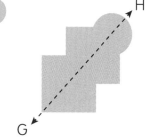 H / G _____

Complete each symmetric figure with the dotted line as a line of symmetry.

9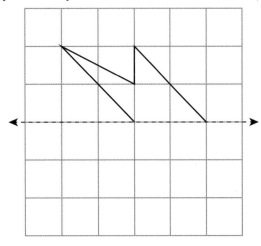

10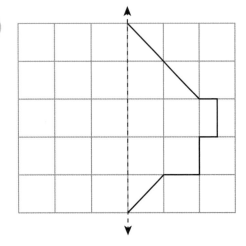

11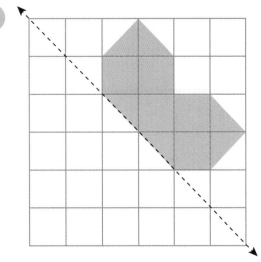

Assessment Prep

Answer each question.

12 Which shapes have at least one pair of parallel sides?
Select all that apply.

Ⓐ

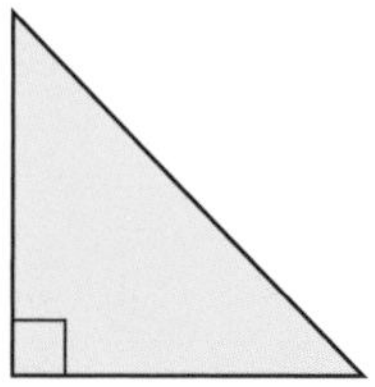

Ⓑ

Ⓒ

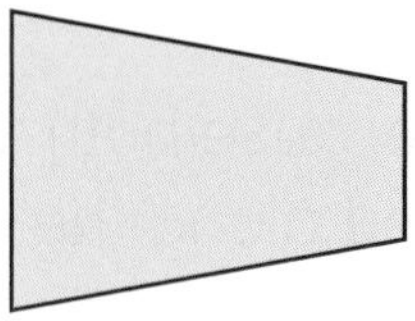

Ⓓ

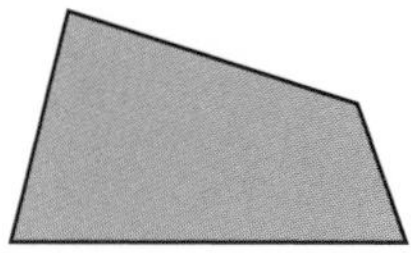

Ⓔ

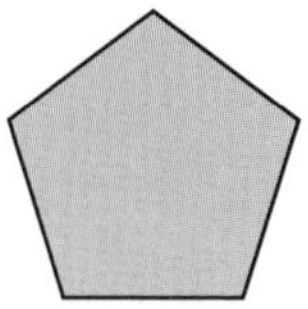

Ⓕ

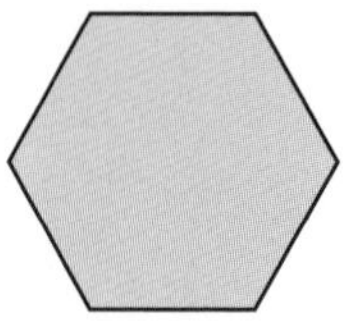

13 Classify the polygon in as many ways as possible. Explain.
Write your answers and explanations in the space below.

14 Tomas says the following is a symmetric shape because both sides of
the shape are equal in shape and size when folded along the dotted
line. Do you agree? Explain.
Write your answer and explanation in the space below.

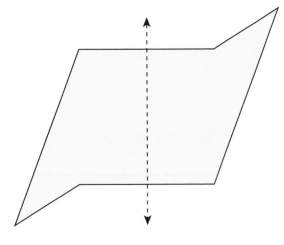

Name: _____ Date: _____

Polygons and Symmetry Around Us

1 Jessica uses polygons to draw a model of a bridge.
Jessica's teacher gave her instructions on how to color the drawing.

a Color the polygons with two pairs of parallel sides blue.
b Color the polygons with one pair of parallel sides green.
c Color the polygons with no parallel sides but with a right angle yellow.
d Color the polygons with no parallel sides and no right angles purple.

Help Jessica color the polygons in her drawing.

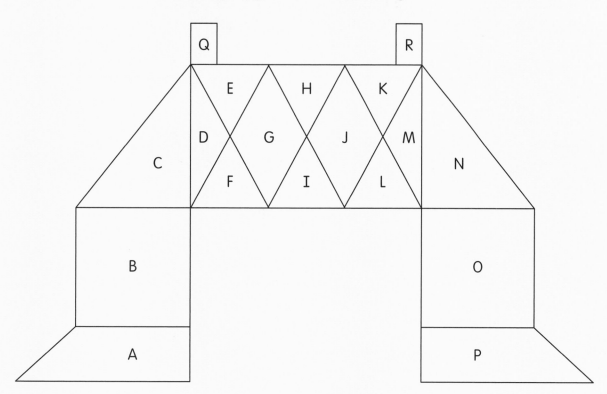

2 Olivia draws a symmetric outline of a building in her school.

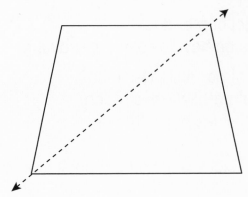

Aisha says, "The dotted line is not a line of symmetry."
Olivia says, "Yes, it is. The dotted line goes right through the middle."
Who is correct, Olivia or Aisha?
Explain your answer.

3 Three students were looking at the name tags on their desks while Ms. Peterson was teaching symmetry.

Student A said, "Each letter in my name has exactly one line of symmetry."

Student B said, "One of the letters in my name has more than one line of symmetry, but the other two letters have only one line of symmetry each."

Student C said, "One of the letters in my name has more than one line of symmetry, but the other two letters don't have any."

TED   ROB   ADI

Identify the three students:

Student A: _____

Student B: _____

Student C: _____

Rubric

Point(s)	Level	My Performance
7–8	4	• Most of my answers are correct. • I showed complete understanding of what I have learned. • I used the correct strategies to solve the problems. • I explained my answers and mathematical thinking clearly and completely.
5–6	3	• Some of my answers are correct. • I showed some understanding of what I have learned. • I used some correct strategies to solve the problems. • I explained my answers and mathematical thinking clearly.
3–4	2	• A few of my answers are correct. • I showed little understanding of what I have learned. • I used a few correct strategies to solve the problems. • I explained some of my answers and mathematical thinking clearly.
0–2	1	• A few of my answers are correct. • I showed little or no understanding of what I have learned. • I used a few strategies to solve the problems. • I did not explain my answers and mathematical thinking clearly.

Teacher's Comments

How can you use a table or a line graph to represent, organize, and interpret information? How do you choose an appropriate graph to show information?

Name: _____ Date: _____

Reading numbers from a number line

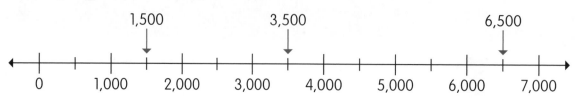

▶ Quick Check

Find each missing number.

1

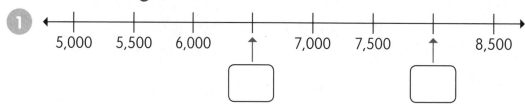

Finding parts of a whole

The tables show the number of apples and oranges sold by two supermarkets one morning.

Supermarket A's Sales

Number of Apples	Number of Oranges	Total Number
19	26	

$19 + 26 = 45$

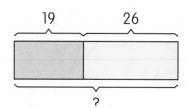

You can find the whole by adding the parts.

Supermarket B's Sales

Number of Apples	Number of Oranges	Total Number
19		45

$$45 - 19 = 26$$

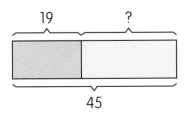

19   ?

45

You can find one part by subtracting the other part from the whole.

▶ **Quick Check**

Find each missing number.

2 ### Number of Vehicles in a Parking Lot

Cars	Motorcycles	Total
32	15	

3 ### Number of People in a School

Students	Teachers	Total
	63	1,342

Interpreting data in a picture graph

The picture graph shows the number of toy cars each student has.

Number of Toy Cars Students Have

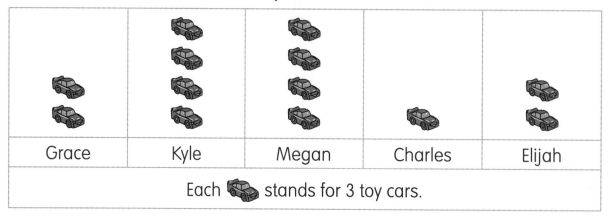

Each 🚗 stands for 3 toy cars.

Elijah has 6 toy cars.
Charles has the fewest toy cars.
Kyle has 12 toy cars. He has the same number of toy cars as Megan.
Grace has 6 fewer toy cars than Kyle.

▶ Quick Check

Use the data in the picture graph to answer each question.

The picture graph shows the favorite fruit of a group of students.

Favorite Fruit of a Group of Students

Each 😃 stands for 4 students.

4 Which fruit was the most popular among the group of students?

_____

5 How many students chose grapes as their favorite fruit?

_____

6 How many more students prefer peaches to melons?

_____

7 How many students were there in the group?

_____

Interpreting data in a bar graph

The bar graph shows the number of visitors at an art show over five days.

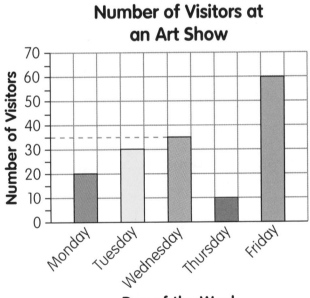

The number of visitors at the art show was greatest on Friday.
The number of visitors at the art show was least on Thursday.
There were 25 fewer visitors on Wednesday than on Friday.
There were 20 more visitors on Tuesday than on Thursday.

▶ **Quick Check**

Use the data in the bar graph to answer each question.

The bar graph shows the number of fundraising tickets sold by volunteers.

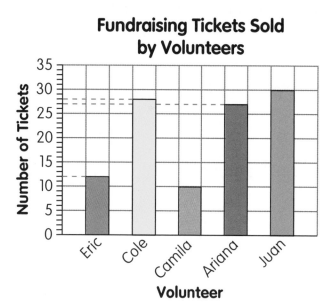

8 Who sold the greatest number of tickets? _____

9 Who sold the least number of tickets? _____

10 How many fewer tickets did Eric sell than Juan? _____

11 Which two volunteers sold a difference of 1 ticket? _____

12 How many tickets did the five volunteers sell altogether? _____

Making and Interpreting a Table

Learning Objectives:
- Make a table from data collected.
- Interpret data in a given table.

THINK

The table shows the lengths of some wires of different colors that are 6.0 centimeters when rounded to the nearest tenth.

Color of wire	Green	Yellow	Blue	Red	Purple
Length of wire	6.03	5.98	?	6.01	?

a The length of the blue wire is the longest possible length, recorded to 2 decimal places. How long is the blue wire?

b The purple wire is the shortest possible length recorded to 2 decimal places. How long is the purple wire?

ENGAGE

Caden asked ten of his friends for their birthday months. He found that three friends were born in January, two were born in February, one was born in March, and four were born in April. Represent the data Caden collected in a bar graph. Discuss with your partner another way to represent the data.

 Make and interpret a table

1 Mr. Cook recorded the favorite subjects and sports of several students.

Jack
📖 English
🏈 Football

Mary
📖 Mathematics
⚾ Baseball

Carlos
📖 Mathematics
🏈 Football

Sara
📖 Science
⚾ Baseball

Bryan
📖 Mathematics
⚾ Baseball

Zoe
📖 English
⚾ Baseball

Ian
📖 Mathematics
🏈 Football

Amelia
📖 Mathematics
🏀 Basketball

Mr. Cook represented the data for the favorite subjects in a table like this.

Favorite Subject	Tally	Number of Students
English	||	2
Mathematics	||||	5
Science	|	1

a The least popular subject is Science.
b The most popular subject is Mathematics.
c 2 students chose English as their favorite subject.
d 4 more students prefer Mathematics to Science.
e Mr. Cook collected the data from 8 students.

You can also present a table in this way. The following table represents the favorite sports of Mr. Cook's students.

Favorite Sport	Football	Baseball	Basketball
Tally	|||	||||	|
Number of Students	3	4	1

Mr. Cook drew a bar graph to represent the data in the table.

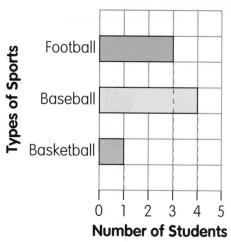

Favorite Sports of Mr. Cook's Students

© 2020 Marshall Cavendish Education Pte Ltd

Hands-on Activity Creating a table

Work in groups of three or four.

1. Ask your classmates how they get to school, and use tally marks to record the data in the tally chart below.

How Students Get to School	Tally
Walk	
Bus	
Car	

2. Count the tally marks and complete the table below.

How Students Get to School	Number
Walk	
Bus	
Car	

③ Write five questions about the data in ② using these words and phrases.

| how many students | fewer | more |
| the least | the most | altogether |

a _____

_____

b _____

_____

c _____

_____

d _____

_____

e _____

_____

TRY Practice making and interpreting a table

Complete the table. Use the data in the table to answer each question.

1. At a class picnic, students brought different kinds of food. Each student brought one food item. The table shows the number of food items the students brought.

Types of Food at the Picnic

Food Item	Tally	Number of Students
Muffins	||||	4
Mini Pies	~~||||~~	
Sandwiches	~~||||~~ |||	
Salad	|||	
Others	~~||||~~ |	

a How many students brought mini pies?

_____

b Which food item did most students bring?

_____

c How many more students brought sandwiches than salad?

_____

d How many students were at the picnic?

_____

Use the data in the table to answer each question.

2 The table shows the pieces of fruits Ms. Watson bought for a party.

Fruit Bought by Ms. Watson

Type of Fruit	Number of Fruit
Apple	10
Orange	20
Peach	5
Apricot	8

a How many oranges did Ms. Watson buy?

_____

b Which type of fruit did Ms. Watson buy the least?

_____

c How many more apricots than peaches did Ms. Watson buy?

_____

d How many pieces of fruits did Ms. Watson buy altogether?

_____

e How many more apricots must Ms. Watson buy if she wants to have the same number of apricots as oranges?

_____

INDEPENDENT PRACTICE

Complete the table. Use the data in the table to answer each question.

1 In a music class, Ms. Cruz asked students to list their favorite music genre, or type of music. The table shows the number of students who listed each genre as their favorite.

Favorite Genres of Ms. Cruz's Students

Music Genre	Tally	Number of Students
Pop	卌 IIII	9
Rock	卌	
Classical	II	
Hip-Hop	IIII	
R&B	卌 III	

a How many students in the class like rock music?

_____

b Which music genre is the most popular among the students?

_____

c How many more students prefer hip-hop music to classical music?

_____

d How many students are there in the music class?

_____

Use the data in the table to answer each question.

2 Each student in a class chose his or her favorite type of pie. The data is represented in the table below.

Type of Pie	Number of Students
Blueberry	12
Lemon	15
Strawberry	8
Apple	22

a How many students chose blueberry pie as their favorite?

_____

b Which type of pie is the least popular among the students?

_____

c How many more students prefer apple pies to lemon pies?

_____

d How many students chose apple pie and strawberry pie as their favorite?

_____

Using a Table

Learning Objective:
- Read and interpret data in a table using the intersections of rows and columns.

New Vocabulary
intersection

 THINK

A television company surveys a group of people to find out which type of program is the most popular among four age groups of people. What do you notice from the information in the table? Why do you think this information is important to the television company? Share your ideas with your partner.

Popular Television Programs

Age Group	Cartoons	Dramas	Documentaries	News
Under 12	769	99	82	50
From 12 to 18	578	201	103	118
From 18 to 30	138	435	169	258
Over 30	104	377	200	319

ENGAGE

The table shows the number of slices of pizzas each stall at the carnival sold and the total amount of money collected.

Stall	Number of Slices Sold	Amount Collected
A	20	$60.00
B	25	$75.00
C	12	$30.60
D	30	$93.00

From the table determine:
a Which stall sold the most pizzas?
b Which stall collected the most money?
c Which stall sold the least expensive slices of pizzas? How do you know?

LEARN Find relevant information in a table

1 Ms. Sanchez is returning home early from a business trip. Help her check the schedule to find a flight leaving for Orange County in the morning.

STEP 2 Column

Flight Schedule

Destination	Departure 9:00 A.M.	Departure 11:00 A.M.	Departure 2:00 P.M.
Salt Lake City	Flight 23	Flight 24	Flight 27
Phoenix	Flight 35	Flight 67	Flight 86
Orange County	Flight 74	Flight 87	Flight 73
San Diego	Flight 63	Flight 26	Flight 98

STEP 1 Row

STEP 3 Intersection

First, look under Destination for the row that shows Orange County.

Then, look across the column headers for a morning departure.

The intersection where the Orange County row meets the 9:00 A.M. column shows Flight 74.

2 The table shows the number of people who watched a movie in a week.

Number of People Who Watched a Movie

Day	Adults	Children	Total Number of People
Monday	160	220	380
Tuesday	?	230	420
Wednesday	210	190	400
Thursday	170	250	420
Friday	250	200	?
Saturday	160	?	280
Sunday	260	220	480

a How many adults watched the movie on Tuesday?

420 – 230 = 190

190 adults watched the movie on Tuesday.

b How many children watched the movie on Saturday?

280 – 160 = 120

120 children watched the movie on Saturday.

c How many more adults than children watched the movie
on Wednesday?

210 – 190 = 20

20 more adults than children watched the movie on Wednesday.

d How many people watched the movie on Friday?

250 + 200 = 450

450 people watched the movie on Friday.

TRY Practice finding relevant information in a table

**Study the rows, columns, and intersections in the table.
Then, fill in each blank.**

The number of medals won by top ranking countries in the 2018 Winter Olympics held in South Korea is recorded in the table.

Medals Won by Top Ranking Countries

Country	Gold	Silver	Bronze	Total
Norway	14	14	11	39
Germany	14	10	7	31
Canada	11	8	10	29
United States	9	8	6	23

1 The United States won _____ gold medals.

2 Canada won a total of _____ medals.

3 Germany won _____ fewer medals than Norway in all.

4 _____ and _____ won the same number of silver medals.

5 The number 7 appears at the intersection of the row for

_____ and the column for _____.

Study the rows, columns, and intersections in the table.
Then, fill in each blank.

A food court surveys customers to find out which type of food is most popular among three age groups of people.

Popular Types of Food

Age Group	Fast Food	Italian	Mexican	Chinese
Under 12	54	21	16	9
From 12 to 18	34	24	29	13
Over 18	11	35	26	28

6 The least number of customers under 12 like _____ food.

7 The greatest number of customers over 18 like _____ food.

8 The difference between the number of customers under 12 who prefer Italian food to Mexican food is _____.

9 The difference between the number of customers in the 12 to 18 age group who prefer fast food to Chinese food is _____.

10 The number of customers over 18 who prefer Mexican and Chinese food is _____ altogether.

Complete the table and answer each question below.

Sophie made this table to show the birthdays of all the students in her class that fell in the months from January to June. All her classmates were born in the same year. Help Sophie complete the table.

Birthday Months of Sophie's Classmates

Birthday Month	Number of Boys	Number of Girls	Total Number
January	2	3	5
February	4		6
March		2	3
April	5		5
May	4	2	
June		3	7
Total			

11 How many classmates were born in May and June?

_____

12 How many classmates were born in these six months?

_____

13 Which month has the greatest number of birthdays?

_____

14 Sophie is the youngest among those born in March.
   a How many of her classmates born from January to June are older than Sophie?

   _____

   b How many of her classmates born from January to June are younger than Sophie?

   _____

Name: _____ Date: _____

INDEPENDENT PRACTICE

Complete the table. Then, fill in each blank.

Ms. Wood recorded her students' favorite colors in a table.

Favorite Colors of Ms. Wood's Students

Color	Number of Boys	Number of Girls	Total Number
Orange	2	4	6
Blue		3	5
Green	3	2	
Yellow	2		4
Total		11	

1 The number 6 appears in the intersection of the row for _____ and the

   column for _____.

2 The number at the intersection of the row for Green and the column for

   Number of Boys is _____.

3 Which color is least popular among the students? _____

4 How many more girls than boys like orange? _____

5 Are there fewer students who like green than orange? _____
   If so, how many fewer? _____

6 What is the total number of boys in the class? _____

7 How many students are there in the class altogether? _____

Complete the table. Answer each question below.

The table shows the number of keychains and magnets sold at each booth during a fundraising event.
Each keychain was sold at $3 and each magnet was sold at $2.

Keychains and Magnets Sold at a Fundraising Event

Booth	Keychain ($3)		Magnet ($2)		Total Amount ($)
	Number of Keychains	Amount Collected ($)	Number of Magnets	Amount Collected ($)	
A	9	27	5	10	37
B	6		6		
C	1		9		
D	4		10		
Total					

8. What was the total amount collected by all the booths?

_____

9. Which booth collected the most money?

_____

10. Which booths sold the greatest number of keychains and magnets in all?

_____

11. Which booth sold the least number of keychains and magnets in all?
Suggest why this booth sold the least number of keychains and magnets.

_____

_____

_____

3 Line Graphs

Learning Objectives:
- Read and interpret line graphs.
- Choose an appropriate graph to display a given data set.

New Vocabulary
line graph
horizontal axis
vertical axis

THINK

Jacob drew a line graph to show the flight of a paper plane he threw. Describe the flight of the paper plane from A to D.

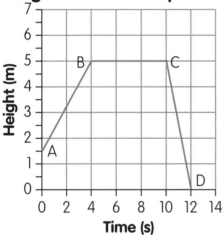

Flight of Jacob's Paper Plane

ENGAGE

Study the graph.

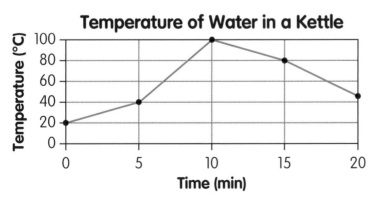

Tell your partner a story using the information provided in the graph.
What does the red line show us?

LEARN Read and interpret a line graph

1 The table shows the temperature at different times of the day at a school.

Temperature at a School

Time	7 A.M.	8 A.M.	9 A.M.	10 A.M.	11 A.M.	12 Noon
Temperature (°F)	70	74	78	84	88	90

The data in the table can also be shown in this line graph.

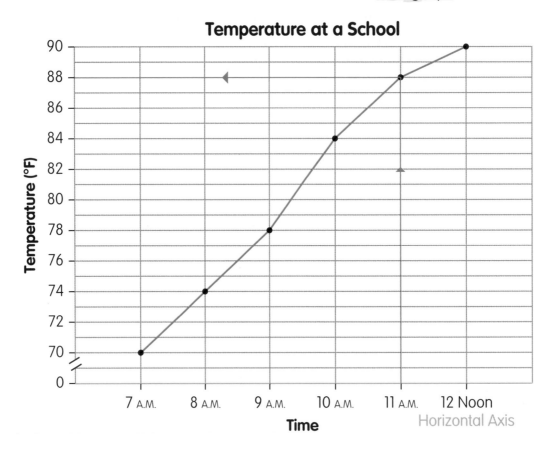

a What is the temperature at 11:00 A.M.?

The red lines track the path of steps 1 to 4. This is how you read the temperature at different times.

STEP 1 Find 11:00 A.M. along the horizontal axis (orange line).

STEP 2 Move up until you meet a point on the graph.

STEP 3 From that point on the graph, move left until you meet the vertical axis (pink line).

STEP 4 The point on the scale, or vertical axis (pink line) is 88°F.

The temperature at 11:00 A.M. is 88°F.

b At what time was the temperature 74°F?

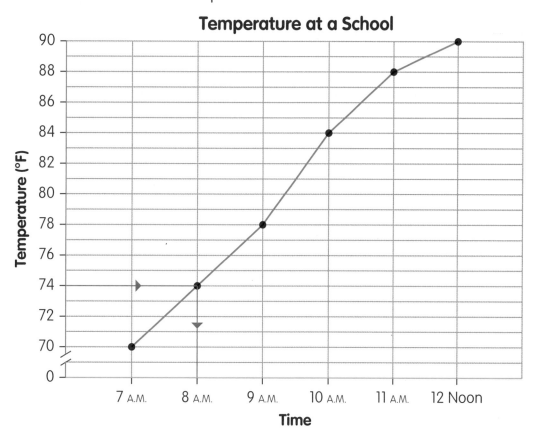

Temperature at a School

The blue lines track the path of steps 1 to 4. This is how you find the time at which the temperature was a given value.

STEP 1 ▶ Find 74°F along the vertical axis.

STEP 2 ▶ Move right until you meet a point on the graph.

STEP 3 ▶ From that point on the graph, move down until you meet the horizontal axis.

STEP 4 ▶ The point on the horizontal axis is 8:00 A.M.

The temperature was 74°F at 8:00 A.M.

TRY Practice reading and interpreting a line graph

Study the table and line graph. Then, answer each question.

The table and line graph show the distance from Diego's home during the first seven minutes of a bus trip.

Distance from Diego's Home

Time after Bus Trip Begins (min)	1	2	3	4	5	6	7
Distance from Diego's Home (m)	250	750	1,250	1,500	1,500	2,500	2,000

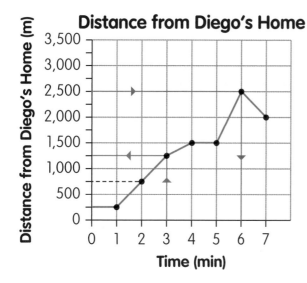

Distance from Diego's Home

1. How far was Diego from his home after 3 minutes on the bus?

    _____

2. After how many minutes was Diego 2,500 meters from his home?

    _____

3. During which 1-minute interval did the bus stop?

    _____

4. What was the increase in distance from Diego's home from the first to the third minute?

    _____

5. After how many minutes did the bus turn around and travel in the direction of Diego's home?

    _____

6. During which 1-minute interval was the bus moving the fastest?

    _____

Study the line graph. Then, fill in each blank.

The line graph shows the cost of a type of wire sold in a hardware store.

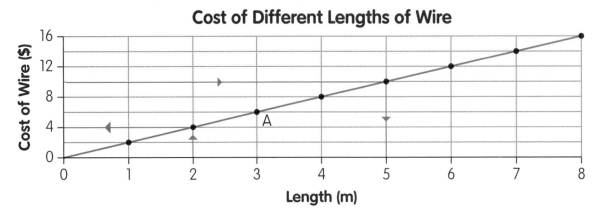

Cost of Different Lengths of Wire

7 a The graph shows that 2 meters of wire cost $ _____.

b The graph also shows that when the cost is $10, the length of the wire is _____ meters.

8 a 4 meters of wire cost $ _____.

b 8 meters of wire cost $ _____.

9 a When the cost is $6, the length of the wire is _____ meters.

b When the cost is $14, the length of the wire is _____ meters.

The graph is a straight line.

10 Find the length and cost of a wire at point A on the graph.

At point A, the length of the wire is _____ meters.

The cost of the wire at point A is $ _____.

11 Use the graph to find the missing numbers below. What is the increase in the cost of the wire for every 1 meter increase in length?

	1 m	1 m	1 m	1 m	Increase in length of wire
Length (m)	1	2	3	4	5
Cost ($)	2	4	_____	_____	10
	$2	_____	_____	_____	Increase in cost of wire

For every 1 meter increase in length, the cost of the wire increases by

$ _____.

Study the line graph. Then, answer each question.

The line graph shows the length of a spring when various masses are hung on it.

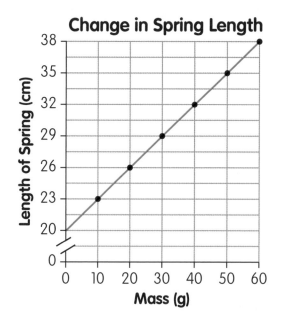

Change in Spring Length

12 What is the length of the spring when it is not stretched? _____

13 What is the length of the spring when these masses are hung on it?

  a 10 grams _____   b 30 grams _____

  c 40 grams _____   d 50 grams _____

14 What is the mass hung on the spring when its length is

  a 26 centimeters? _____   b 38 centimeters? _____

15 Compare the original length of the spring to its length when different masses are hung on it.

  a By how many centimeters is the spring stretched when a mass of

     60 grams is hung on it? _____

  b If the spring is stretched by 15 centimeters, what is the mass that

     is hung on it? _____

ENGAGE

Jennifer recorded the height of a plant over five months.

Month	Height of Plant (cm)
April	5
May	7
June	11
July	14
August	20

Jennifer wants to represent the data in a graph. Which graph do you think she should choose — a picture graph, a bar graph, or a line graph? Explain your reasoning to your partner.

LEARN Choose an appropriate graph to represent data

1 Alex wrote a report on Nature Park for a class project. He used different types of graphs to show data about the park in different ways.

a Alex wanted to compare the number of people who visited the park on different days of the week. He used a bar graph to show this data.

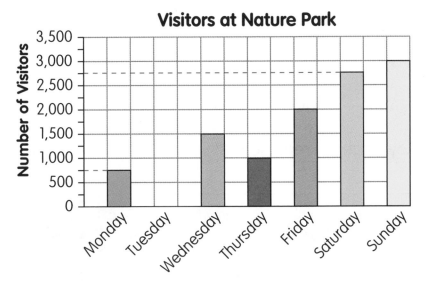

There were more visitors at Nature Park on Sunday than on any other day.
On Tuesday, there were no visitors at the park.
There were 500 more visitors on Friday than on Wednesday.

A bar graph is useful for comparing data, especially when the numbers are large.

We can show any number on a bar graph by choosing an appropriate scale.

b Alex then surveyed 48 visitors to find out the best month to visit the park. He used a picture graph to show the results.

Best Month to Visit Nature Park

Key: Each ⭐ represents 3 visitors.

A picture graph is useful for showing data with numbers that are multiples of a certain number. In a picture graph, use a key instead of a scale.

15 visitors chose April as the best month to visit Nature Park. The same number of visitors chose March and July as combined, the best months to visit Nature Park.

Both bar graphs and picture graphs are useful for comparing data. A picture graph is more suitable for showing data with smaller numbers. However, a bar graph is useful for showing data with small as well as large numbers.

In a picture graph, it is hard to show numbers that are not exact multiples of a certain number. In a bar graph, we can show any number with an appropriate scale.

c   Alex used a line graph to show how the temperature at the park changed over a few hours.

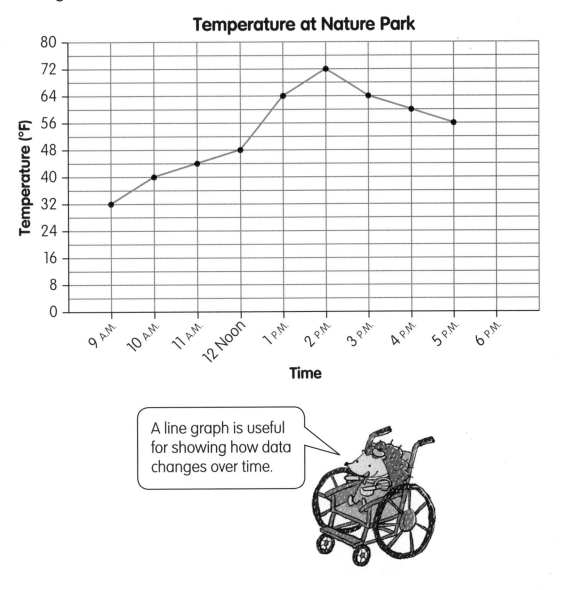

Temperature at Nature Park

A line graph is useful for showing how data changes over time.

The highest temperature was recorded at the park at 2:00 P.M. The temperature at the park increased from 9:00 A.M. to 2:00 P.M., and then decreased.

The greatest increase in the temperature was between 12 Noon and 1:00 P.M.

TRY Practice choosing an appropriate graph to represent data

Choose a graph to display each data set. Fill in each blank with bar graph, line graph, or picture graph.

1 A comparison of the number of visitors to an art museum in six different months

Visitors at an Art Museum

Month	January	February	March	April	May	June
Number of Visitors	230	80	340	630	420	540

A _____ can be used to compare data when the numbers are large.

2 The number of books read by some students each month

Number of Books Read by Students

Student	Liam	Henry	Faith	Paige
Number of Books	12	8	16	4

A _____ can be used when the numbers are small, and are multiples of a certain number.

3 Nathan's mass over five months

Nathan's Mass

Month	January	February	March	April	May
Mass (kg)	22	25	26	24	23

A _____ can be used to show how data changes over time.

INDEPENDENT PRACTICE

Use the data in the line graph to answer each question.

The line graph shows the height of a balloon above the ground between 1:00 P.M. and 6:00 P.M. on Monday.

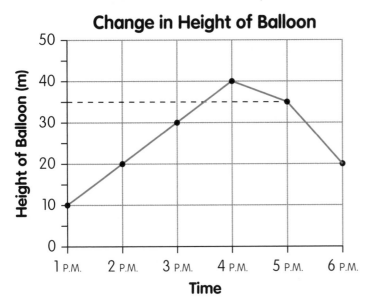

1 What was the height of the balloon at
   a 1:00 P.M.?

   _____

   b 5:00 P.M.?

   _____

2 What was the greatest height the balloon reached?

   _____

   At what time did it reach the height?

   _____

3 In which 1-hour interval did the greatest decrease in height occur?

   _____

4 What was the difference between the greatest and lowest heights reached by the balloon?

   _____

Choose a graph to display each data set. Write bar graph, line graph, or picture graph. Explain your choice.

Ms. Kim, the school librarian, collected these sets of data. Help her select the most suitable graph for each data set.

5 Ms. Kim wants the principal to see the difference in the number of visitors to the library in the first few weeks of the year.

Visitors to the Library

Week	1	2	3	4	5	6
Number of Visitors	300	180	260	340	420	150

_____

_____

6 Ms. Kim asked 30 Grade 1 students for their favorite books so that she could plan the Young Readers' Program.

Favorite Books

Category	Adventure	Science Fiction	Mystery	Fairy Tales
Number of Students	6	3	6	15

_____

_____

7 Ms. Kim wants to show how the number of students at the library changes during the day.

Number of Students at the Library

Time	9 A.M.	11 A.M.	1 P.M.	3 P.M.
Number of Students	20	28	35	12

_____

_____

Name: _____ Date: _____

Mathematical Habit 2 Use mathematical reasoning

Mr. Lee owns a flower shop. The table and line graph show his earnings over five days.

Daily Earnings

Day	1	2	3	4	5
Earnings ($)	540	680	620	760	660

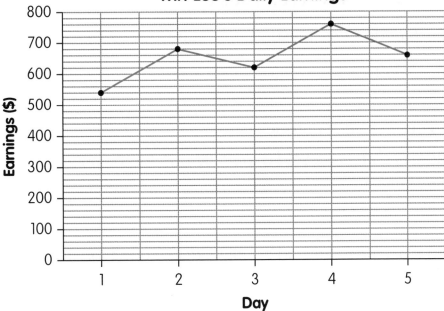

Is it easier to tell how Mr. Lee's earnings changed over the five days from the table or the line graph? Explain.

_____

_____

_____

_____

1 **Mathematical Habit 1** Persevere in solving problems

The tables show the number of ears of corn sold at two farm stands from Monday to Thursday last week.

Corn Sales at Farm Stand A

Day	Monday	Tuesday	Wednesday	Thursday
Number Sold	125	150	180	240

Corn Sales at Farm Stand B

Day	Monday	Tuesday	Wednesday	Thursday
Number Sold	160	235	110	185

Use the tables to answer each question.

a How many ears of corn were sold at both stands combined on Tuesday?

b How many ears of corn were sold at both stands combined from Monday to Thursday?

c On which days did Stand A sell more corn than Stand B?

d On which days did Stand A sell more than 150 ears of corn?

e On which days did Stand B sell more than 180 ears of corn?

f How many more ears of corn would Stand A have to sell on Tuesday in order to match the number of ears of corn sold by Stand B on the same day?

2 | **Mathematical Habit 2** Use mathematical reasoning

The graph shows the height of the water level in a water dispenser over 7 hours.

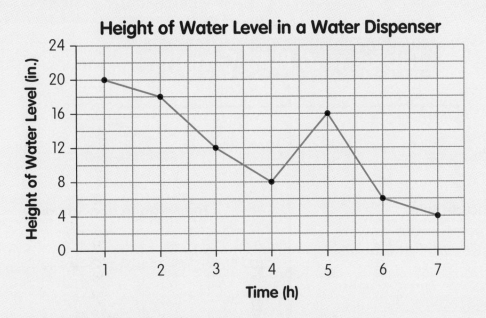

Height of Water Level in a Water Dispenser

a During which 1-hour interval was the decrease in the height of the water level the greatest?

b What do you think happened between the fourth and fifth hour? Explain.

CHAPTER WRAP-UP

How can you use a table or a line graph to represent, organize, and interpret information? How do you choose an appropriate graph to show information?

Tables and Line Graphs

Tables

Bicycle Sales

Day	Bicycle Sales
Monday	5
Tuesday	6
Wednesday	10
Thursday	1
Friday	3

Most bicycles were sold on Wednesday.

Twice as many bicycles were sold on Tuesday than on Friday.

22 bicycles were sold in all from Monday to Thursday.

Line

Temperature at a School

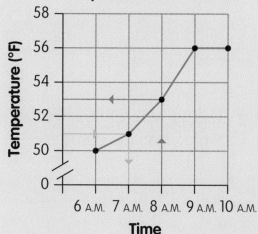

The lowest temperature was recorded at 6 A.M.

There was no change in temperature from 9 A.M. to 10 A.M.

Choosing an Appropriate Graph

- A bar graph is useful for comparing data, especially when the numbers are large.

- A picture graph is useful for comparing data when the numbers are small, and are multiples of a certain number.

- A line graph is used to show how data changes over time.

Name: _____ Date: _____

**Count the tally marks and complete the table.
Then, use the table to answer each question.**

Dominic collects data on the number of siblings his classmates have.

1. **Number of Siblings of Dominic's Classmates**

Number of Siblings	Tally	Number of Students
0	卌 ‖	
1	卌 卌 ‖	
2	卌 ‖	
3	‖	
4		

2. How many of Dominic's classmates have 4 siblings?

_____

3. How many more of Dominic's classmates have 2 siblings than 3 siblings?

_____

4. How many siblings do most of his classmates have?

_____

5. How many of Dominic's classmates have fewer than 2 siblings?

_____

6. How many classmates did Dominic collect data from altogether?

_____

Use the table to answer each question.

A clothing store surveys customers to find out which item in the store is the most popular among three age groups of people.

Popular Items in a Clothing Store

Age Group	T-shirts	Sweaters	Jeans	Jackets
Under 18	38	21	31	10
From 18 to 25	28	24	30	18
Over 25	23	21	24	32

7 The greatest number of people under 18 buy _____.

8 The least number of people over 25 buy _____.

9 The difference between the number of people in the 18 to 25 age group who prefer the sweaters to the jackets in the store is _____.

10 The clothing store surveyed _____ people over 25 altogether.

11 The number of people who buy T-shirts and jeans altogether is _____.

Use the line graph to answer each question.

The line graph shows the distance Clara jogged in a week.

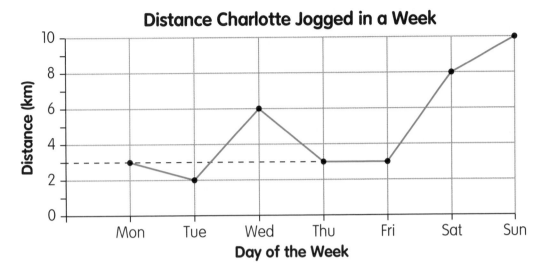

12 On which day did Clara jog the greatest distance?

_____

13 On which day did Clara jog the shortest distance?

_____

14 On which day did Clara jog twice as far as she did on Thursday?

_____

15 What is the difference between the distance Clara jogged on Wednesday and on Sunday?

_____

Choose a graph to display each data set. Write bar graph, line graph, **or** picture graph. **Explain your choice.**

16 A grocer wants to know how her earnings have changed over four months.

The Grocer's Earnings

Month	June	July	August	September
Amount Earned ($)	3,500	2,750	3,800	3,600

_____

_____

17 A toy store wants to find out which is the most popular item and the least popular item in the store during the week.

Number of Items Sold at the Toy Store

Item	Soft Toys	Train Sets	Building Blocks Set	Board Games
Number of Items	480	640	720	320

_____

_____

18 A coach records the number of points scored by the players on the basketball team during a game.

Number of Points Scored During a Game

Player	Gianna	Andrea	Maya	Rachel	Bailey
Number of Points	3	8	12	5	2

_____

_____

Assessment Prep

Answer each question.

Use the data in the table to answer Part A and Part B.
Four classes from Michael's Elementary School collected dimes and quarters during a fundraising event. The table shows the number of dimes and quarters that each class collected.

Dimes and Quarters Collected at a Fundraising Event

Class	Number of Dimes	Number of Quarters	Total Number
4-1	34	40	74
4-2	30	28	58
4-3	27	?	62
4-4	38	23	61

Part A

19 How many quarters did Class 4-3 collect?

(A) 23

(B) 27

(C) 28

(D) 35

Part B

20 How many dimes and quarters did the four classes collect in all?
Show your work.

Write your answer and your work in the space below.

The line graph shows the amount of gas Ms. Long used from January to May.

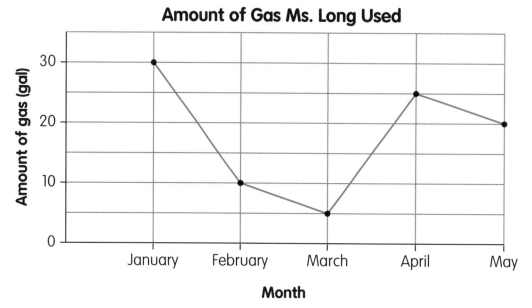

Amount of Gas Ms. Long Used

21 What is the difference between the greatest amount of gas used and the least amount of gas used? Show your work.

Write your answer and your work in the space below.

Name: _____ Date: _____

Fundraising Event

1 Rogers Elementary School held a sale, selling scones to raise money for the fourth grade students.
On the first day of the sale, the students sold 102 glazed scones, 73 almond scones, 67 maple scones, 82 buttermilk scones, 58 blueberry scones, and 42 cheese scones.

a Complete the table below.

First Day of the Sale

Type of Scone	Number Sold

b Which type of scone sold was more than twice as many as the least popular scone?

c What was the total number of scones sold on the first day of the sale?

d If the students sold two scones for $1, how much money would they make on the first day of the sale?

2 The graphs show the number of scones sold on the first day of the sale.

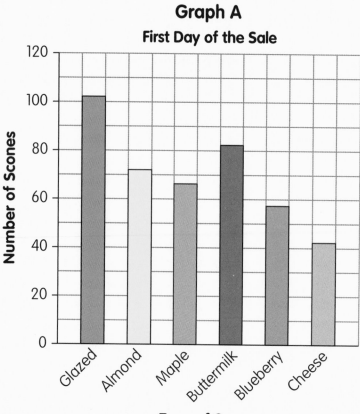

Graph A

First Day of the Sale

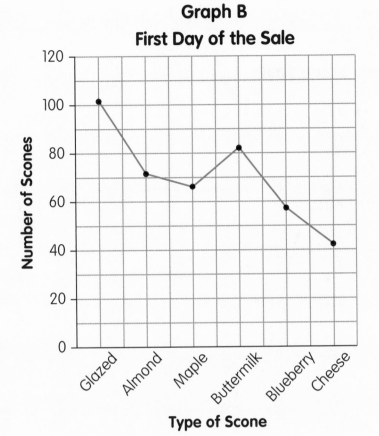

Graph B
First Day of the Sale

a Which graph displays the data from the table better?

Graph A or Graph B? _____

b Explain your answer in a.

3 The line graph shows the number of scones sold during each hour on the first day of the sale.

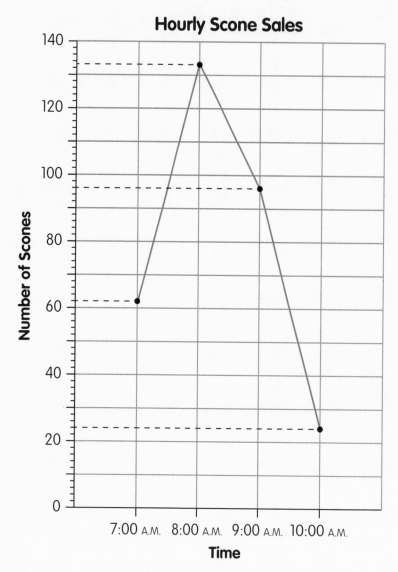

Hourly Scone Sales

a At what time did the students sell the most number of scones?

b The school will have an assembly on the next day.
Based on the bar graph, when would be the best time to hold the assembly in order not to disrupt sales? Why?

Rubric

Point(s)	Level	My Performance
7–8	4	• Most of my answers are correct. • I showed complete understanding of what I have learned. • I used the correct strategies to solve the problems. • I explained my answers and mathematical thinking clearly and completely.
5–6	3	• Some of my answers are correct. • I showed some understanding of what I have learned. • I used some correct strategies to solve the problems. • I explained my answers and mathematical thinking clearly.
3–4	2	• A few of my answers are correct. • I showed little understanding of what I have learned. • I used a few correct strategies to solve the problems. • I explained some of my answers and mathematical thinking clearly.
0–2	1	• A few of my answers are correct. • I showed little or no understanding of what I have learned. • I used a few strategies to solve the problems. • I did not explain my answers and mathematical thinking clearly.

Teacher's Comments

Glossary

A

- **acute angle**

  An angle with a measure less than 90°.

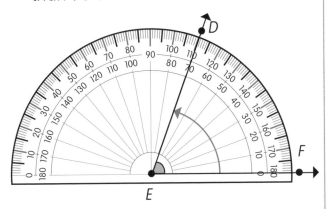

∠*DEF* is an acute angle.

- **acute triangle**

  A triangle with three acute angles.

B

- **base (of a drawing triangle)**

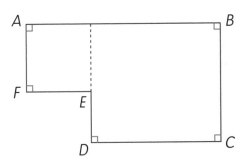

The straightedge is at the base of the drawing triangle.

C

- **composite figure**

Figure *ABCDEF* is a composite figure. It can be broken up into a square and a rectangle.

- **cup (c)**

  A customary unit of capacity.
  1 cup = 8 fl oz

D

- **degrees (in angles)**

  A unit of angle measure. An angle measure is a fraction of a full turn. The symbol for degrees is °.

  A right angle has a measure of 90 degrees. It can be written as 90°.

- **distance**

  Distance is a numerical measurement of how far apart objects are.

- **drawing triangle**

  An instrument used to draw perpendicular and parallel line segments.

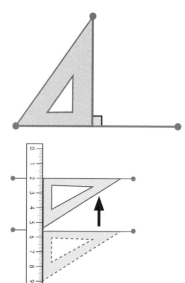

- **fluid ounce (fl oz)**

  A customary unit of capacity.
  1 fl oz $= \frac{1}{8}$ cup

- **formula**

  A mathematical rule that shows the relationship between two or more values.

- **gallon (gal)**

  A customary unit of capacity.
  1 gal = 16 cups

- **horizontal axis**

  The x-axis on a graph.

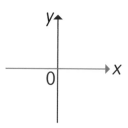

- **inner scale (of a protractor)**

  The inner set of readings on a protractor used for measuring angles.

  Since $\overrightarrow{EF}$ passes through the zero mark of the inner scale, read the measure on the inner scale.

  Measure of $\angle DEF = 70°$

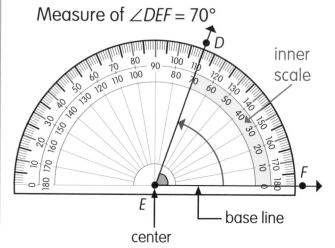

- **intersection**

  The meeting point of two things.

Set 1 / Set 2	A	B	C	D
W				
X				
Y			Q	
Z				

  The alphabet Q appears in the <u>intersection</u> of row Y and column C.

K

- **kilometer (km)**

  A metric unit of distance.
  1 km = 1,000 m

L

- **line graph**

  A graphical display of information that changes continuously over time.

- **line of symmetry**

  A line that divides a figure into two congruent parts. The parts match exactly when folded along this line.

  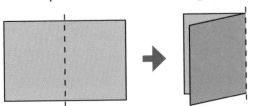

M

- **mile (mi)**

  A customary unit of distance.
  1 mi = 5,280 ft

O

- **obtuse angle**

  An angle with a measure greater than 90° but less than 180°.

  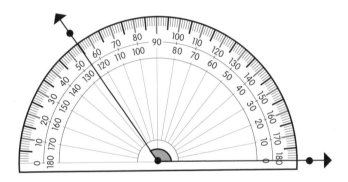

  $\angle f$ is an obtuse angle.

- **obtuse triangle**

  A triangle with one obtuse angle.

- **ounce (oz)**

  A customary unit of weight.
  $1 \text{ oz} = \frac{1}{16} \text{ lb}$

outer scale (of a protractor)

The outer set of readings on a protractor used for measuring angles.

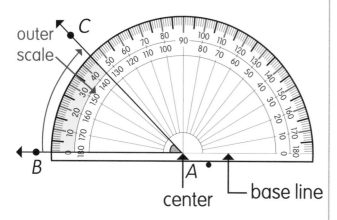

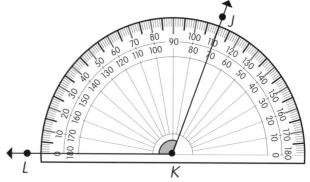

Since $\overrightarrow{AB}$ passes through the zero mark of the outer scale, read the measure on the outer scale.

Measure of $\angle CAB = 45°$

P

pint (pt)

A customary unit of capacity.
1 pt = 2 cups

pound (lb)

A customary unit of weight.
1lb = 16 oz

protractor

An instrument used to measure and draw angles.

Q

quart (qt)

A customary unit of capacity.
1 qt = 4 cups

R

ray

A ray is part of a line that continues without end in one direction. It has one endpoint.

Letters can be used to name a ray. The first letter is always the endpoint.

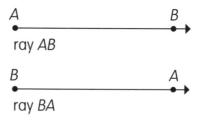

Ray AB can also be written as $\overrightarrow{AB}$, and ray BA as $\overrightarrow{BA}$.

- **right triangle**

  A triangle with exactly one right angle.

  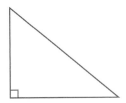

- **second (s)**

  A unit of time. $1\text{ s} = \frac{1}{60}$ min

- **straight angle**

  An angle with a measure of 180°.

  180°

- **symmetric shape**

  A symmetric shape has two parts that match each other along the line of symmetry.

  A symmetric shape can have more than one line of symmetry.

  line of symmetry

  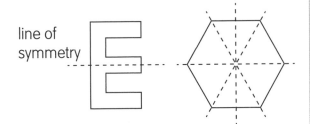

- **symmetric pattern**

  We can create symmetric patterns on square grid paper.

  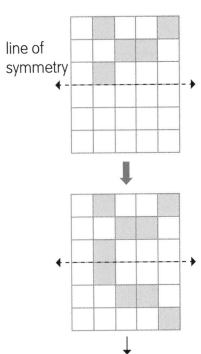

  line of symmetry

  This is a symmetric pattern.

- **turns (and right angles)**

  1 right angle

  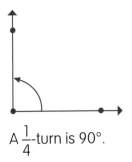

  A $\frac{1}{4}$-turn is 90°.

2 right angles

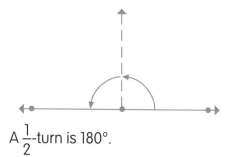

A $\frac{1}{2}$-turn is 180°.

3 right angles

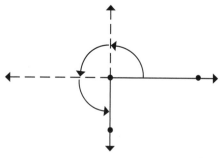

A $\frac{3}{4}$-turn is 270°.

4 right angles

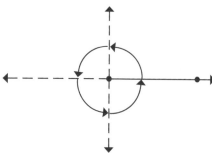

A full turn is 360°.

- **ton (T)**

  A customary unit of weight.
  1 ton = 2,000 lb

- **vertical axis**

  The y-axis on a graph.

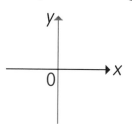

- **yard (yd)**

  A customary unit of length.
  1 yd = 3 ft

Index

A

B

C

> Pages in **boldface** type shows where a term is introduced.

lines of, **274**, 273, 279, 290, 298
patterns, *see* Symmetric patterns
shapes, *see* Symmetric shapes

Photo Credits

1: linux87/ 123rf.com, 1r: vejaa/ 123rf.com, 2: pixelrobot/ 123rf.com, 2: Vitalii Artiushenko/ 123rf.com, 2: © Elisabeth Burrell | Dreamstime.com/ dreamstime.com, 3: rangizzz/ 123rf.com, 3: Gcapture/ dreamstime. com, 3: mtsaride/ 123rf.com, 4: pakhnyushchyy/ 123rf.com, 4: orson/ 123rf.com, 4: fotyma/ 123rf.com, 5: Elnur Amikishiyev/ 123rf.com, 5: creativecommonsstockphotos/ dreamstime.com, 5: 123rfaurinko/ 123rf.com, 6: serezniy/ 123rf.com, 6: Keith Homan/ 123rf.com, 6: Denismart/ dreamstime.com, 7: Данил Снигирев/ 123rf. com, 9: Charcharist Dararuang/ dreamstime.com, 13: tiero/ 123rf.com, 19: 123rf.com, 19: Natis76/ dreamstime. com, 20: 123rf.com, 20tr: creativecommonsstockphotos/ dreamstime.com, 20: utima/ 123rf.com, 20: Natis76/ dreamstime.com, 20b: creativecommonsstockphotos/ dreamstime.com, 21: creativecommonsstockphotos/ dreamstime.com. 21: orson/ 123rf.com, 21 dreamstime.com, 21: nito500/ 123rf.com 21: belchonock/ 123rf. com, 22: diana taliun/ 123rf.com, 22: Somchai Jongmeesuk/ 123rf.com, 22: creativecommonsstockphotos/ dreamstime.com, 22: pixelrobot/ 123rf.com, 23: Sergii Telesh/ 123rf.com, 23: Bert Folsom/ 123rf.com, 24: Natis76/ dreamstime.com, 24: wiml/ 123rf.com, 25: Alexander Raths/ 123rf.com, 26: 123rf.com, 26: Miraswonderland/ dreamstime.com, 26: Elnur Amikishiyev/ 123rf.com, 27: Natis76/ dreamstime.com, 27: Andrey Eremin/ /23rf.com, 27: tinnko/ 123rf.com, 28: Evgenyi Lastochkin/ 123rf.com, 29: Konstantinos Moraitis/ 123rf.com, 29: okolaa/ 123rf. com, 29: Siwaporn Tharawattanatham/ 123rf.com, 29: andrelix/ 123rf.com, 29: Gergana Valkova/ 123rf.com, 31: blueringmedia/ 123rf.com, 32: Marusea Turcu/ dreamstime.com, 49: Maksym Bondarchuk/ dreamstime. com, 50: Jacek Sopotnicki/ dreamstime.com, 52: Stangot/ dreamstime.com, 95: Anton Starikov/ 123rf.com, 100: Wrangel | Dreamstime.com/ dreamstime.com, 100: Esther Aleman/ 123rf.com, 101: gnohz/ 123rf.com, 101: Christin Farmer/ dreamstime.com, 122: Velveteye1/ dreamstime.com, 128: Kitthanes Ratanasira Anan/ 123rf.com, 141: Jacques Durocher/ 123rf.com, 171: Jan Janu/ dreamstime.com, 171: dvarg/ 123rf.com, 171: Pedro Campos/ 123rf. com, 174tl: © MCE, 174tm: © MCE, 174tr: © MCE, 174mb: © MCE, 176: © MCE, 178: Egasit Mullakhut/dreamstime. com, 178: Chakrapong Worathat/ 123rf.com, 178: photka/ 123rf.com, 180: Vvoevale/ dreamstime.com, 222: costasz/ 123rf.com, 255: NATTEE CHALERMTIRAGOOL/ 123rf.com, 282: andreykuzmin/ 123rf.com, 293: fwstudio/ freepik.com, 309: Veronika Ilieva/ 123rf.com, 322: Annie Zhak/ dreamstime.com, 322: Brig4nti/ dreamstime. com, 322: Dmytro Tolmachov/ dreamstime.com, 322: David Cabrera Navarro/ dreamstime.com, 345: fwstudio/ freepik.com

NOTES

NOTES

NOTES

NOTES

NOTES

© 2020 Marshall Cavendish Education Pte Ltd

Published by Marshall Cavendish Education
Times Centre, 1 New Industrial Road, Singapore 536196
Customer Service Hotline: (65) 6213 9688
US Office Tel: (1-914) 332 8888 | Fax: (1-914) 332 8882
E-mail: cs@mceducation.com
Website: www.mceducation.com

Distributed by
Houghton Mifflin Harcourt
125 High Street
Boston, MA 02110
Tel: 617-351-5000
Website: www.hmhco.com/programs/math-in-focus

First published 2020

ISBN 978-0-358-10185-7

Printed in Singapore

2 3 4 5 6 7 8   1401   25 24 23 22 21 20
4500799762   B C D E F

The cover image shows an Angolan giraffe.
Giraffes can be found in many African countries, out on the open plains. A giraffe's long neck allows it to reach up high to feed on new leaf shoots at the top of trees. Giraffes live in herds and can run fast to get away from lions and other predators. They sleep for about four hours a day.